The Greatest Historical Warriors

The Greatest Historical Warriors

Hseham Amrahs

mds0

1

Alexander the Great (Greece)

Alexander the Great stands as one of the most legendary figures in history, renowned for his military conquests, strategic brilliance, and enduring legacy. Born in 356 BCE in Pella, the ancient capital of Macedonia, Alexander ascended to the throne at a young age and went on to create one of the largest empires the world had ever seen. His unparalleled military campaigns reshaped the political landscape of the ancient world and left an indelible mark on civilizations for centuries to come.

Birth

Alexander, son of King Philip II of Macedon and Queen Olympias, entered the world in 356 BCE. His birth was accompanied by auspicious omens, including the burning of the Temple of Artemis in Ephesus, which was interpreted as a sign of his future greatness. From an early age, Alexander displayed remarkable intelligence, courage, and ambition, qualities that would shape his destiny as a conqueror and visionary leader.

Early Life and Education

Alexander received a rigorous education under the tutelage of the renowned philosopher Aristotle. Under Aristotle's guidance, he studied a wide range of subjects, including philosophy, science, literature, and warfare. These formative years instilled in Alexander a love of learning and a thirst for knowledge that would accompany him throughout his life.

Wars

Alexander's military campaigns are legendary and form the cornerstone of his legacy. Upon ascending to the throne of Macedonia in 336 BCE following his father's assassination, Alexander wasted no time in asserting his authority and expanding his empire.

One of Alexander's earliest and most significant conquests was the defeat of the Persian Empire. In 334 BCE, he led his army across the Hellespont into Asia Minor, marking the beginning of his epic Persian campaign. Over the next decade, Alexander achieved a series of stunning victories against the Persian forces, including the decisive battles of Issus and Gaugamela. His military genius and tactical brilliance allowed him to overcome seemingly insurmountable odds and conquer vast stretches of territory.

Alexander's conquests extended far beyond the borders of the Persian Empire. He marched eastward into the heart of Asia, subjugating kingdoms and founding new cities along the way. His legendary journey took him as far as India, where he defeated the formidable king Porus at the Battle of the Hydaspes in 326 BCE.

Despite his military successes, Alexander faced numerous challenges and setbacks throughout his campaigns. He encountered fierce resistance from local populations, logistical difficulties, and mutinies among his troops. However, his unwavering determination and charismatic leadership enabled him to overcome these obstacles and continue his relentless march of conquest.

Cultural and Educational Reforms

In addition to his military exploits, Alexander is also remembered for his contributions to culture and learning. He sought to spread Greek culture and civilization throughout the lands he conquered, a process known as Hellenization. He encouraged the blending of Greek and local traditions, fostering a spirit of cultural exchange and mutual understanding.

Alexander's conquests facilitated the spread of Greek language, art, and philosophy across the ancient world, laying the foundations for the Hellenistic age that followed his reign. He founded numerous cities, many of which bore his name, including the famed Alexandria in Egypt. These cities served as centers of learning and commerce, promoting intellectual exchange and innovation.

Death

Tragically, Alexander's life was cut short at the age of 32. In 323 BCE, after a decade of conquest and expansion, he fell ill suddenly and died in Babylon. The exact cause of his death remains a subject of debate among historians, with theories ranging from natural causes to assassination. Regardless of the circumstances, Alexander's passing marked the end of an era and left a power vacuum that would lead to the fragmentation of his empire.

Interesting Facts and Figures

- Alexander's empire spanned three continents and covered over two million square miles, making it one of the largest in history.
- He is said to have tamed the legendary steed Bucephalus at the age of 12, a feat that showcased his bravery and equestrian skills.
- Alexander's military campaigns resulted in the spread of Greek culture and the fusion of Greek and Eastern traditions, a phenomenon known as the Hellenistic synthesis.
- He is credited with founding over 20 cities, many of which became major cultural and commercial centers in the ancient world.
- Alexander's conquests inspired countless legends and myths, cementing his status as a legendary figure in history.

Overall Win and Lose

Alexander the Great's legacy is one of triumph and conquest, tempered by the challenges and complexities of empire-building. He transformed the ancient world through his military campaigns, spreading Greek culture and civilization to the farthest reaches of his empire.

Despite his untimely death, Alexander's vision and ambition continue to inspire admiration and fascination to this day. While his empire eventually fragmented in the wake of his passing, his enduring legacy as one of history's greatest conquerors remains firmly etched in the annals of time.

2

Alfred the Great (England)

Alfred the Great, born in 849 in Wantage, England, is a towering figure in English history. He ruled as King of Wessex from 871 until he died in 899. Alfred is remembered not only for his military prowess but also for his cultural and educational reforms, earning him the epithet "the Great." His reign marked a pivotal moment in English history, as he defended his kingdom against Viking invasions and laid the groundwork for a unified England.

Birth

Alfred was born in 849, the youngest son of King Æthelwulf of Wessex and Osburh. Though he was not initially expected to inherit the throne, fate had other plans for him. Even in his youth, Alfred displayed qualities of leadership and intelligence that would define his reign as king.

Early Life and Education

Alfred's early years were marked by turmoil and Viking raids. He received a basic education, learning to read and write in Old English, Latin, and some Welsh. He showed a keen interest in literature, history, and religion from a young age, which would later shape his vision for a more educated kingdom.

Wars

The Viking invasions that plagued England during Alfred's lifetime presented the greatest challenge of his reign. In 865, the Great

Heathen Army, led by the sons of the legendary Viking Ragnar Lothbrok, descended upon England, sacking cities and laying waste to the countryside. Alfred's kingdom of Wessex faced relentless attacks from these Norse warriors.

Despite early setbacks, Alfred proved to be a resilient and strategic leader. He implemented military reforms, building fortified towns known as burhs and organizing a system of militia known as the fyrd. These measures allowed him to defend Wessex against Viking incursions and launch counteroffensives to reclaim lost territory.

One of Alfred's most significant victories came in 878 at the Battle of Edington, where he decisively defeated the Great Heathen Army led by Guthrum. This victory secured Wessex and paved the way for a period of relative peace in the region. Alfred's military successes earned him the admiration of his subjects and solidified his reputation as a great warrior king.

Cultural and Educational Reforms

Beyond his military achievements, Alfred's reign is also remembered for his efforts to promote learning and culture. Recognizing the importance of education in building a strong and prosperous society, Alfred took steps to revive scholarship in his kingdom.

He translated several Latin works into Old English, including historical texts and religious works. Perhaps most notably, Alfred commissioned the compilation of the Anglo-Saxon Chronicle, a historical record of England from the time of Julius Caesar's invasion to the ninth century. This chronicle provided invaluable insight into the history of England and helped preserve its cultural heritage.

Alfred also founded schools and monasteries, inviting scholars from across Europe to teach in his kingdom. He sought to elevate the intellectual and moral standards of his subjects, believing that a well-educated populace was essential for the prosperity and stability of his realm.

Death

Alfred the Great passed away on October 26, 899, at the age of 50. His death marked the end of an era and left a lasting legacy that would shape the course of English history for centuries to come. He was succeeded by his son, Edward the Elder, who continued his father's work of consolidating and expanding the kingdom of Wessex.

Interesting Facts and Figures

- Alfred was the only English monarch to be given the title "the Great."
- He is credited with laying the foundations for the English legal system and promoting the use of English as a language of government.
- Alfred was a devout Christian and sought to instill Christian values in his kingdom. He translated several religious texts into Old English for the benefit of his subjects.
- Despite his many achievements, Alfred faced numerous challenges during his reign, including bouts of illness and the constant threat of Viking attacks.
- Alfred was known for his sense of justice and fairness, earning him the respect and loyalty of his subjects.

Overall Win and Lose

Alfred the Great's reign can be characterized as a period of both triumph and adversity. Despite facing relentless Viking invasions and internal strife, Alfred emerged as a resilient and visionary leader who successfully defended his kingdom and laid the foundations for a unified England. His military victories, cultural reforms, and commitment to education earned him a place among the greatest monarchs in English history. While he faced setbacks and challenges along the way, Alfred's enduring legacy continues to inspire generations of Englishmen and women.

3

Ashoka the Great (India)

Ashoka the Great, also known as Ashoka the Maurya, is one of India's most celebrated emperors. His reign, which spanned from 304 to 232 BCE, marked a significant period of Indian history characterized by both conquest and enlightenment. Ashoka's legacy is defined not only by his military conquests but also by his embrace of Buddhism and his commitment to promoting peace, tolerance, and social welfare throughout his vast empire.

Birth

Ashoka was born in 304 BCE, the son of Emperor Bindusara and Queen Dharma. He was born into the Maurya dynasty, which ruled over the Indian subcontinent from its capital at Pataliputra (modern-day Patna). From a young age, Ashoka displayed intelligence, courage, and ambition, traits that would shape his reign as emperor.

Early Life and Education

Ashoka received a princely education befitting his royal status. He was well-versed in the art of warfare, administration, and statecraft. However, it was his exposure to Buddhism that would have the most profound impact on his life and reign. Ashoka's conversion to Buddhism played a central role in shaping his policies and worldview, leading him to adopt a philosophy of non-violence and compassion.

Wars

Ashoka's reign was marked by a series of military campaigns that expanded the boundaries of his empire and solidified his power. One of his most famous conquests came in 261 BCE with the annexation of the Kalinga region (modern-day Odisha) in eastern India. The conquest of Kalinga was a bloody affair, resulting in significant loss of life and devastation. The suffering he witnessed on the battlefield deeply affected Ashoka and prompted a profound spiritual transformation.

Following the conquest of Kalinga, Ashoka underwent a period of introspection and soul-searching. He was filled with remorse over the violence and bloodshed unleashed by his conquests. In a famous edict, known as the Kalinga Edict, Ashoka expressed his deep regret for the suffering caused by the war and declared his commitment to ruling with compassion and benevolence.

Cultural and Educational Reforms

One of Ashoka's most enduring legacies is his promotion of Buddhism and his efforts to spread its teachings throughout his empire. He erected numerous stupas, monasteries, and pillars inscribed with edicts proclaiming his commitment to Buddhist principles. Ashoka also dispatched emissaries to neighboring kingdoms and beyond to propagate the Dhamma (Buddhist teachings) and promote religious tolerance.

In addition to his religious reforms, Ashoka implemented a wide range of social welfare measures aimed at improving the lives of his subjects. He established hospitals, veterinary clinics, and rest houses for travelers along major trade routes. He also promoted the welfare of animals, issuing edicts against hunting and cruelty to animals.

Death

Ashoka passed away in 232 BCE after ruling for nearly 40 years. His death marked the end of a remarkable reign characterized by both conquest and enlightenment. He was succeeded by his son, Dasaratha, though the Maurya Empire would gradually decline in the centuries following Ashoka's death.

Interesting Facts and Figures

- Ashoka's empire encompassed much of the Indian subcontinent, stretching from present-day Afghanistan in the west to Bangladesh in the east.
- He is credited with constructing the Great Stupa at Sanchi, one of the oldest and most important Buddhist monuments in India.
- Ashoka's edicts, inscribed on pillars and rocks throughout his empire, provide valuable insights into his policies and beliefs.
- He is said to have sent Buddhist missionaries to Sri Lanka, Southeast Asia, and even as far as Greece and Egypt.
- Ashoka's reign is considered a golden age in Indian history, characterized by peace, prosperity, and cultural flourishing.

Overall Win and Lose

Ashoka the Great's legacy is one of profound transformation and enlightenment. Despite his early military conquests, he ultimately rejected violence and embraced a philosophy of non-violence and compassion. His conversion to Buddhism and his commitment to promoting peace and social welfare set him apart as a visionary leader whose influence extended far beyond the boundaries of his empire.

While Ashoka's military campaigns expanded the reach of his empire, it was his commitment to Dhamma and his efforts to promote tolerance and understanding that truly defined his reign. His legacy continues to resonate in India and beyond, serving as a reminder of the enduring power of compassion and the potential for positive change in the world.

4

Attila the Hun (Hunnic Empire)

Attila the Hun, often referred to as the "Scourge of God," was a fearsome and enigmatic ruler who led the Hunnic Empire during the turbulent period of the late 4th and early 5th centuries. His name evokes images of barbarian hordes sweeping across Europe, leaving destruction in their wake. Attila's military prowess, diplomatic cunning, and ruthless ambition made him one of the most formidable figures of his time, and his legacy continues to fascinate historians and storytellers to this day.

Birth

Attila was born around 406, the son of Mundzuk, a chieftain of the Hunnic tribes, and his wife. Little is known about Attila's early life, but he likely spent his formative years on the harsh steppes of Central Asia, where he honed his skills as a warrior and leader.

Early Life and Rise to Power:

Attila's rise to power began in the aftermath of the death of his uncle, King Rugila, in 434. Alongside his brother Bleda, Attila assumed leadership of the Hunnic Empire, forging alliances with neighboring tribes and consolidating his authority over the vast Hunnic confederation.

Under Attila's leadership, the Huns emerged as a dominant force on the Eurasian steppes, exacting tribute from surrounding peoples and launching raids deep into Roman territory. His shrewd diplomatic maneuvering and formidable military strength enabled him to expand his influence and build a reputation as a fearsome adversary.

Wars

Attila's military campaigns were characterized by their ferocity and ruthlessness. He launched multiple invasions of the Eastern Roman Empire, plundering cities and laying waste to the countryside. In 441, he signed the Treaty of Margus with the Eastern Roman Empire, securing vast territories in the Balkans in exchange for an annual tribute.

However, Attila's ambitions extended far beyond the borders of the Roman Empire. In 445, he launched a devastating invasion of the Eastern Roman Empire, besieging Constantinople and ravaging Thrace and the Balkans. The following years saw Attila continue his campaigns of conquest, raiding as far west as Gaul and Italy.

One of Attila's most infamous campaigns came in 451 when he invaded Gaul (modern-day France) with a massive army. The Roman general Flavius Aetius, along with his Visigothic allies led by King Theodoric I, met Attila in battle near the Catalaunian Plains. The resulting Battle of the Catalaunian Plains was a brutal and bloody conflict that ended in a tactical stalemate, with neither side able to claim a decisive victory.

Despite his setback in Gaul, Attila continued to pose a significant threat to the Roman Empire. In 452, he launched a second invasion of Italy, besieging the city of Aquileia and threatening Rome itself. Legend has it that Pope Leo I intervened and persuaded Attila to spare the city, though the exact circumstances of this meeting remain a subject of debate among historians.

Death

Attila's death in 453 marked the end of an era of Hunnic dominance in Europe. According to historical accounts, he died suddenly on his wedding night, possibly as a result of a burst blood vessel or alcohol poisoning. With Attila's passing, the unity of the Huns began to unravel, and the empire soon descended into chaos and infighting.

Interesting Facts and Figures

- Attila's empire stretched from the steppes of Central Asia to the plains of Eastern Europe, encompassing a vast territory and a diverse array of peoples.
- He was known for his fearsome appearance, with contemporary accounts describing him as having a large head, flat nose, and small, deep-set eyes.
- Attila was a master of psychological warfare, using fear and intimidation to subdue his enemies and extract tribute from conquered peoples.
- He was a skilled diplomat as well as a warrior, forging alliances with rival tribes and playing off the competing interests of the Eastern and Western Roman Empires.
- Attila's legacy as the "Scourge of God" continues to loom large in popular culture, inspiring countless legends, myths, and works of fiction.

Overall Win and Lose

Attila the Hun's legacy is one of both triumph and tragedy. As one of the most formidable military leaders of his time, he carved out a vast empire and struck fear into the hearts of his enemies. His campaigns of conquest reshaped the political landscape of Europe and left an indelible mark on history.

However, Attila's relentless pursuit of power and wealth ultimately proved to be his downfall. Despite his military successes, he was unable to achieve his ultimate goal of conquering Rome and establishing himself as the undisputed ruler of the Western world. His death in 453 marked the beginning of the decline of the Hunnic Empire and paved the way for the rise of other powers in Europe.

In the end, Attila's legacy is a complex and multifaceted one. While he is remembered as a fearsome warrior and a symbol of barbarian savagery, he also played a significant role in shaping the course of European history. His legacy continues to be debated and reevaluated by historians, ensuring that the name of Attila the Hun will be remembered for generations to come.

5

Bajirao I (India)

Bajirao I, also known as Bajirao Ballal, was a renowned military general and statesman who served as the Peshwa (Prime Minister) of the Maratha Empire from 1720 to 1740. His exceptional military acumen, strategic brilliance, and administrative reforms earned him a place as one of the greatest figures in Indian history. Bajirao's campaigns expanded the Maratha Empire to its zenith, solidifying its position as a dominant force in the Indian subcontinent during the 18th century.

Birth

Bajirao was born in 1700 in the town of Shirdi, located in present-day Maharashtra, India. He was born into the prestigious Peshwa family, which held significant political and military influence within the Maratha Empire. From a young age, Bajirao displayed exceptional intelligence, leadership qualities, and a deep understanding of military strategy.

Early Life and Education

Bajirao received a comprehensive education befitting his noble lineage. He was trained in the art of warfare, politics, diplomacy, and administration under the guidance of his father, Balaji Vishwanath, who served as the first Peshwa of the Maratha Empire. Bajirao's upbringing prepared him for the challenges he would face as a military leader and statesman in a tumultuous period of Indian history.

Wars

Bajirao's military career was characterized by a series of brilliant campaigns and conquests that expanded the territory and influence of the Maratha Empire. One of his most notable achievements came early in his career when he led a successful campaign against the Mughal Empire in Malwa in 1723. This victory established Bajirao as a formidable military leader and earned him widespread acclaim throughout the Maratha Empire.

Throughout his tenure as Peshwa, Bajirao launched several military campaigns to expand Maratha's influence and secure its borders. His most famous campaign came in 1737 when he led an expedition to the north to confront the Nizam of Hyderabad, who had encroached upon Maratha territory. Bajirao's forces achieved a decisive victory at the Battle of Bhopal, securing the Maratha Empire's control over the region.

Bajirao's military genius was further demonstrated in his innovative tactics and strategies on the battlefield. He pioneered the use of guerrilla warfare, mobility, and speed to outmaneuver larger enemy forces, earning him the nickname "The Thunderbolt" (Bajirao) for his swift and devastating attacks.

Cultural and Administrative Reforms:

In addition to his military achievements, Bajirao is also remembered for his administrative reforms and contributions to Maratha culture. He implemented measures to improve governance, streamline taxation, and promote trade and commerce within the empire. Bajirao also patronized the arts and literature, fostering a cultural renaissance that enriched Maratha society.

Under Bajirao's leadership, the Maratha Empire reached its zenith, extending its influence from the Deccan plateau to the north and northwest regions of India. His administrative reforms laid the groundwork for the empire's continued prosperity and stability in the years to come.

Death

Tragically, Bajirao's life was cut short at the age of 40 when he succumbed to a sudden illness in 1740. His death was a great loss to the Maratha Empire, depriving it of one of its greatest leaders and military strategists. Bajirao was succeeded as Peshwa by his eldest son, Balaji Bajirao, who would continue his father's legacy of expansion and consolidation.

Interesting Facts and Figures

- Bajirao's military campaigns expanded the Maratha Empire to its greatest territorial extent, encompassing large parts of present-day India.
- He is credited with introducing several military innovations, including the use of light cavalry and rapid maneuvering tactics.
- Bajirao's love story with Mastani, the daughter of a Rajput king, has been romanticized in Indian folklore and popular culture.
- He was known for his ascetic lifestyle and simple habits, despite his lofty position as Peshwa of the Maratha Empire.
- Bajirao's legacy as a military genius and visionary leader continues to inspire admiration and reverence in India.

Overall Win and Lose

Bajirao I's legacy is one of triumph and achievement, marked by his remarkable military successes, administrative reforms, and contributions to Maratha culture and society. Through his strategic brilliance and leadership, he expanded the Maratha Empire to its greatest territorial extent and secured its position as a dominant force in the Indian subcontinent.

While Bajirao faced challenges and setbacks during his reign, including conflicts with rival powers and internal dissent, his enduring legacy as one of India's greatest military leaders remains firmly entrenched in history. His innovative tactics, administrative reforms, and cultural patronage continue to shape the legacy of the Maratha Empire and inspire generations of Indians to this day.

6

Belisarius (Byzantine Empire)

Belisarius, one of the most distinguished generals in Byzantine history, epitomizes the military prowess and strategic brilliance of the Eastern Roman Empire during the reign of Emperor Justinian I. Born in 505, Belisarius rose from humble origins to become a legendary figure renowned for his military conquests, tactical innovations, and unwavering loyalty to the Byzantine Empire. His campaigns reshaped the geopolitical landscape of the Mediterranean world and left an indelible mark on the history of the Byzantine Empire.

Birth

Belisarius was born around 505 AD in Germania, a small town in Thrace, part of the Byzantine Empire. Little is known about his early life or family background, but he likely came from a modest background, with no noble lineage to boast of. Despite his humble origins, Belisarius would go on to achieve greatness on the battlefield and earn a place among the most celebrated generals in Byzantine history.

Early Life and Education

Belisarius received a basic education, likely learning to read and write in Greek, the lingua franca of the Byzantine Empire. However, it was on the battlefield where he truly excelled, demonstrating exceptional skill and bravery as a soldier from a young age. Belisarius quickly rose through the ranks of the Byzantine army, earning a reputation for his military acumen and leadership abilities.

Wars

Belisarius' military career was marked by a series of brilliant campaigns and conquests that solidified the Byzantine Empire's control over its territories and expanded its influence abroad. One of his most notable achievements came in the early 530s when he led a successful campaign against the Vandal Kingdom in North Africa.

The Vandalic War fought between 533 and 534, saw Belisarius lead a small but highly disciplined Byzantine force across the Mediterranean to challenge the Vandals, who had established a powerful kingdom in North Africa. Through a combination of bold strategic maneuvers and tactical brilliance, Belisarius defeated the Vandals in a series of battles, culminating in the capture of their capital, Carthage, in 534. This victory restored North Africa to Byzantine control and dealt a significant blow to the Vandal Kingdom.

Following his success in North Africa, Belisarius was tasked with confronting the Ostrogothic Kingdom in Italy. The Gothic War fought between 535 and 554, saw Belisarius lead Byzantine forces in a protracted conflict against the Ostrogoths, who had established themselves as rulers of Italy following the fall of the Western Roman Empire.

Belisarius' campaigns in Italy were marked by both triumphs and setbacks. He achieved notable victories, including the capture of key cities such as Naples, Rome, and Ravenna. However, internal divisions within the Byzantine Empire, as well as the arrival of reinforcements for the Ostrogoths, prolonged the war and made it difficult for Belisarius to achieve a decisive victory.

Despite these challenges, Belisarius' military genius and perseverance enabled him to maintain Byzantine control over much of Italy. However, his efforts were ultimately undermined by the political machinations of the Byzantine court and the lack of sufficient reinforcements and resources. In 554, Belisarius was recalled to Constantinople, leaving Italy in a state of instability and uncertainty.

Cultural and Administrative Reforms:

While Belisarius is best known for his military exploits, he also played a significant role in shaping the cultural and administrative landscape of the Byzantine Empire. As a trusted advisor to Emperor Justinian I, Belisarius participated in the implementation of various reforms aimed at strengthening the empire's institutions and promoting its cultural and intellectual life.

Belisarius advocated for measures to improve the administration of conquered territories, promote economic development, and ensure the welfare of the empire's subjects. He also supported initiatives to preserve and promote Greek culture and learning, fostering a cultural renaissance that enriched Byzantine society.

Death

Belisarius died in 565, at the age of 60. The exact circumstances of his death are unclear, but he is believed to have passed away peacefully in Constantinople. Despite his many accomplishments, Belisarius' later years were marked by political intrigue and personal trials, as he fell out of favor with Emperor Justinian I and faced accusations of treason and conspiracy.

Interesting Facts and Figures

- Belisarius was known for his humility and integrity, earning him the respect and admiration of his soldiers and contemporaries.
- He was married to Antonina, a woman of considerable influence and ambition who played a significant role in his life and career.
- Belisarius' campaigns in North Africa and Italy showcased his mastery of both land and naval warfare, as well as his ability to adapt to changing circumstances on the battlefield.
- Despite his military successes, Belisarius faced numerous challenges and setbacks throughout his career, including political intrigue, rivalries within the Byzantine court, and insufficient resources and support from the imperial government.

- Belisarius' legacy as one of the greatest generals in Byzantine history continues to be celebrated in literature, art, and popular culture.

Overall Win and Lose

Belisarius' military career was marked by both triumphs and tribulations. While he achieved remarkable victories in North Africa and Italy, securing Byzantine control over key territories and expanding the empire's influence abroad, his later years were marred by political intrigue and personal trials.

Despite his many accomplishments, Belisarius was ultimately unable to overcome the challenges posed by internal divisions within the Byzantine Empire, as well as the limitations imposed by the imperial court. His legacy as one of the greatest generals in Byzantine history endures, however, serving as a testament to his skill, bravery, and unwavering dedication to the empire he served.

7

Blackbeard (England)

Blackbeard, whose real name was Edward Teach or Thatch, is one of the most infamous and feared pirates in history. Active during the early 18th century, Blackbeard terrorized the seas of the Caribbean and the eastern coast of North America, plundering merchant ships and spreading fear wherever he sailed. His fearsome appearance, strategic cunning, and ruthless tactics earned him a notorious reputation that has persisted for centuries.

Birth

Edward Teach, later known as Blackbeard, is believed to have been born around 1680 in Bristol, England. Little is known about his early life, including his family background or upbringing. Some historians speculate that he may have served as a privateer during Queen Anne's War before turning to piracy.

Early Life and Education

Blackbeard's early life remains shrouded in mystery, with few details available about his upbringing or education. It is believed that he began his career as a sailor, possibly serving aboard merchant ships or privateer vessels. His experiences at sea would have provided him with the skills and knowledge necessary to become a successful pirate captain later in life.

Piracy and Notoriety:

Blackbeard's piracy career began in the early 18th century when he joined the crew of Benjamin Hornigold, a notorious pirate operating in the Caribbean. Under Hornigold's tutelage, Blackbeard quickly rose through the ranks, demonstrating leadership abilities and a penchant for daring raids.

In 1716, Blackbeard seized control of a French slave ship, which he renamed Queen Anne's Revenge, and outfitted it with cannons and other weaponry. With his newly acquired flagship, Blackbeard embarked on a series of audacious raids along the eastern seaboard of North America, plundering merchant vessels and terrorizing coastal communities.

Blackbeard's fearsome reputation was further enhanced by his imposing appearance and flamboyant demeanor. He was known for wearing multiple pistols and knives strapped to his chest and for weaving slow-burning fuses into his long beard, which he lit during battle to create a terrifying spectacle. These tactics were intended to strike fear into the hearts of his enemies and make them more likely to surrender without a fight.

Wars

Blackbeard's piracy career coincided with a period of widespread lawlessness and conflict known as the Golden Age of Piracy. During this time, European powers vied for control of the lucrative trade routes of the Caribbean and the Americas, leading to frequent clashes between pirates, privateers, and naval forces.

Blackbeard's most famous exploits occurred during the War of the Spanish Succession (1701-1714), a conflict between European powers over the Spanish throne. As tensions escalated, piracy flourished in the Caribbean, with pirates like Blackbeard taking advantage of the chaos to plunder merchant ships and disrupt colonial trade.

One of Blackbeard's most infamous acts came in 1717 when he blockaded the port of Charleston, South Carolina, demanding a ransom in exchange for sparing the city from attack. His audacious actions struck fear into the hearts of colonial authorities and demonstrated the extent of his power and influence.

Death

Blackbeard's reign of terror came to an end in 1718 when he was killed in a dramatic naval battle off the coast of North Carolina. A joint expedition led by Lieutenant Robert Maynard of the Royal Navy and colonial forces from Virginia cornered Blackbeard's ship, the Adventure, in Ocracoke Inlet.

The ensuing battle was fierce and bloody, with Blackbeard and his crew putting up a fierce resistance. Despite being outnumbered, Blackbeard fought ferociously, sustaining multiple gunshot wounds before finally succumbing to his injuries. Legend has it that Blackbeard was decapitated by Maynard's men, who then displayed his severed head on the bow of their ship as a grisly trophy.

Interesting Facts and Figures

- Blackbeard's fearsome reputation and legendary exploits have made him a popular figure in popular culture, inspiring numerous books, films, and television shows.
- He is believed to have amassed a considerable fortune during his piracy career, though much of it remains undiscovered to this day.
- Blackbeard's name and reputation struck fear into the hearts of sailors and coastal communities throughout the Caribbean and the Americas.
- He was known for his strategic cunning and ability to outmaneuver naval forces, earning him the respect and admiration of his fellow pirates.
- Despite his ruthless reputation, Blackbeard was known to show mercy to his captives on occasion, often releasing them unharmed after plundering their ships.

Overall Win and Lose

Blackbeard's piracy career was characterized by both triumphs and defeats. While he achieved considerable success as a pirate captain, amassing a fortune and striking fear into the hearts of his enemies, his reign of terror ultimately came to a violent end at the hands of naval forces in 1718.

Though Blackbeard's death marked the end of his piracy career, his legend lived on, inspiring fear and fascination for generations to come. His exploits continue to capture the imagination of historians, writers, and filmmakers, ensuring that the name of Blackbeard will forever be associated with the Golden Age of Piracy.

8

Boudica (Celtic Britons)

Boudica, also spelled Boadicea, stands as one of the most iconic figures in ancient British history. As a queen of the Celtic Iceni tribe, she rose to prominence during a tumultuous period of Roman conquest and colonization in Britain. Boudica's leadership and bravery in the face of Roman oppression have immortalized her as a symbol of resistance and defiance against imperial domination.

Birth

The exact date and place of Boudica's birth are unknown, as historical records from this period are scarce. However, she is believed to have been born around the mid-1st century CE, possibly in the territory of the Iceni tribe, located in present-day Norfolk, England. Little is known about her early life or family background, but she would later emerge as a fierce and influential leader.

Early Life and Education

Boudica likely received an upbringing typical of noble Celtic women of her time, which would have included training in household management, agriculture, and perhaps some knowledge of warfare and leadership. Although specific details about her education are scarce, Boudica's later actions suggest that she possessed a keen intellect, strong leadership qualities, and a deep sense of loyalty to her people and their traditions.

Wars

Boudica's rise to prominence came in 60 or 61 CE when her husband, Prasutagus, the king of the Iceni tribe, died under mysterious circumstances. According to Roman historian Tacitus, Prasutagus had been a client king of Rome, but upon his death, the Romans seized control of his kingdom and subjected the Iceni to harsh treatment and exploitation.

Infuriated by the Romans' actions, Boudica emerged as a charismatic and determined leader, rallying her people and neighboring tribes to revolt against their oppressors. Together with the Trinovantes, another Celtic tribe, Boudica led a massive uprising against Roman rule, igniting a conflict that would become known as the Boudican Revolt.

Boudica's forces launched a series of devastating attacks on Roman settlements and military outposts throughout the southeastern region of Britain. The Roman historian Cassius Dio describes the brutality of the revolt, with Boudica's forces reportedly slaughtering thousands of Roman citizens and allies, including women and children, and burning cities to the ground.

One of the most infamous incidents of the revolt occurred in 60 or 61 CE when Boudica's forces sacked the Roman provincial capital of Camulodunum (modern-day Colchester) and laid waste to the city, exacting brutal revenge on the Roman inhabitants. They then marched on to Londinium (modern-day London) and Verulamium (modern-day St. Albans), where they perpetrated similar acts of destruction and violence.

Despite their initial successes, Boudica's rebellion ultimately ended in defeat. In 61 CE, a Roman army under the command of Governor Gaius Suetonius Paulinus confronted Boudica's forces in a decisive battle somewhere in the Midlands of England, possibly near present-day Leicester or Birmingham.

The Battle of Watling Street, as it came to be known, was a bloody and brutal affair, with Boudica's forces suffering a crushing defeat at the hands of the well-disciplined and heavily armed Roman legions. According to historical accounts, tens of thousands of Celtic warriors were killed in the battle, and Boudica herself is said to have perished, either by suicide or in combat.

Death

The exact circumstances of Boudica's death remain uncertain, as historical accounts vary in their details. According to Tacitus, Boudica either died from illness or poisoned herself to avoid capture by the Romans following her defeat at the Battle of Watling Street. Another account by Cassius Dio suggests that Boudica fell in battle alongside her warriors, refusing to surrender to the Romans.

Regardless of the specifics, Boudica's death marked the end of her rebellion and the suppression of Celtic resistance to Roman rule in Britain. While her revolt ultimately failed to overthrow Roman domination, Boudica's legacy as a symbol of British resistance and national pride endured for centuries to come.

Interesting Facts and Figures

- Boudica's name is believed to be derived from the Celtic word "bouda," meaning "victory."
- She is often depicted in historical accounts and artistic representations as a powerful and fierce warrior queen, leading her people into battle against the Roman oppressors.
- Boudica's rebellion was one of the largest and most significant uprisings against Roman rule in Britain, highlighting the deep-seated grievances and resistance among the Celtic tribes.
- The exact number of casualties and the extent of the destruction caused by Boudica's revolt are difficult to ascertain, but historical sources describe widespread devastation and loss of life.
- Boudica's story has inspired numerous works of literature, art, and film, cementing her status as a legendary figure in British history.

Overall Win and Lose

Boudica's rebellion against Roman rule in Britain was ultimately unsuccessful, ending in defeat and the suppression of Celtic resistance. Despite her initial victories and the widespread devastation caused by her revolt, Boudica's forces were unable to withstand the disciplined and well-equipped Roman legions in open battle.

However, Boudica's legacy as a symbol of defiance and national pride endured long after her death. Her courage, determination, and willingness to fight against overwhelming odds have inspired generations of Britons to stand up against tyranny and oppression. Today, Boudica remains a revered figure in British history, celebrated for her bravery and unwavering commitment to her people and their freedom.

9

Charles Martel (France)

Charles Martel, often known as the "Hammer," was a powerful Frankish statesman and military leader who played a pivotal role in shaping the course of European history during the early Middle Ages. Born into a prominent noble family, Charles rose to prominence as the de facto ruler of the Frankish realm, successfully defending it against external threats and laying the foundation for the Carolingian dynasty's rise to power.

Birth

Charles Martel was born around 688 CE in Herstal, in present-day Belgium. He was the illegitimate son of Pepin of Herstal, the Mayor of the Palace of Austrasia, and a noblewoman named Alpaida. Despite being born out of wedlock, Charles would go on to become one of the most influential figures of his time, leaving an indelible mark on the history of Europe.

Early Life and Education

Little is known about Charles Martel's early life and education. Growing up in the tumultuous political landscape of early medieval Europe, he likely received military training and education in the arts of war and governance befitting his noble status. Charles would later prove himself as a capable and cunning leader on the battlefield and in the political arena.

Wars

Charles Martel's military career was defined by his leadership during the Muslim conquests in Western Europe and his pivotal role in repelling the Islamic invasion at the Battle of Tours in 732 CE. The Muslim armies, led by Abdul Rahman Al Ghafiqi, had crossed the Pyrenees into Gaul (modern-day France) and were advancing northward, pillaging and plundering Christian territories along the way.

Recognizing the imminent threat posed by the Muslim invaders, Charles Martel assembled a Frankish army and marched to confront the Muslim forces near the city of Tours in central France. The two armies clashed in a fierce and decisive battle that would determine the fate of Western Europe.

The Battle of Tours, fought on October 10, 732 CE, was a pivotal moment in European history. Despite being outnumbered, Charles Martel's forces, consisting of heavily armored Frankish infantry and mounted cavalry, held their ground against the Muslim cavalry charges and infantry assaults. The disciplined and well-equipped Frankish army proved to be a formidable opponent for the Muslim warriors, who were unaccustomed to fighting in the rugged terrain of Western Europe.

After a day of intense fighting, the Muslim forces, exhausted and demoralized, began to retreat from the battlefield. Charles Martel seized the opportunity to launch a decisive counterattack, driving the retreating Muslim armies from the field and securing a resounding victory for the Franks. The Battle of Tours is often cited as a turning point in the Muslim conquests in Western Europe and is credited with halting the advance of Islam into the heart of the continent.

Death

Charles Martel died on October 22, 741 CE, in Quierzy-sur-Oise, France. His death marked the end of an era of Frankish leadership and military prowess, but his legacy lived on through his descendants and the Carolingian dynasty that he helped to establish.

Interesting Facts and Figures

- Charles Martel's nickname, "Martel," which means "the Hammer" in Old French, was likely given to him as a testament to his military prowess and his ability to crush his enemies on the battlefield.
- He is considered one of the founding figures of the Carolingian dynasty, which would go on to produce some of the most influential rulers in European history, including Charlemagne.
- Charles Martel's victory at the Battle of Tours is often romanticized in European history as a triumph of Christian civilization over the forces of Islam, although modern historians debate the extent of its significance in halting Muslim expansion in Western Europe.
- Despite his military successes, Charles Martel faced challenges from rival factions within the Frankish realm, including conflicts with his family members over control of the kingdom.
- Charles Martel's legacy as a strong and decisive leader continues to be celebrated in French history and culture, with numerous monuments and memorials dedicated to his memory.

Overall Win and Lose

Charles Martel's victory at the Battle of Tours secured his place in history as one of the most important figures of the early Middle Ages. By repelling the Muslim invaders and halting their advance into Western Europe, he safeguarded Christian civilization and preserved the cultural and political identity of the Frankish realm.

Although Charles Martel faced internal conflicts and challenges during his rule, his military prowess and leadership ultimately prevailed, laying the foundation for the rise of the Carolingian dynasty and the emergence of Charlemagne as one of the most powerful rulers in European history. His legacy as the "Hammer of the Franks" endures as a symbol of strength, courage, and resilience in the face of adversity.

10

Ching Shih (China)

Ching Shih, also known as Cheng I Sao, was a formidable pirate queen who commanded the most powerful fleet in Chinese maritime history. Rising from humble beginnings as a prostitute, she became a legendary figure in the early 19th century, terrorizing the South China Sea and challenging the might of imperial navies. Ching Shih's remarkable leadership, strategic acumen, and sheer audacity have immortalized her as one of the most successful pirates in history.

Birth

Ching Shih was born in 1775 in the Guangdong province of southern China. Little is known about her early life, including her birth name and family background. She entered the world of piracy through unconventional means, setting in motion a remarkable journey that would see her rise to unprecedented heights of power and influence.

Early Life and Education

As a young woman, Ching Shih worked as a prostitute in a brothel in Canton (modern-day Guangzhou), where she caught the eye of Cheng I, a notorious pirate captain. Impressed by her intelligence and beauty, Cheng I took Ching Shih as his wife and made her an integral part of his pirate crew.

Under Cheng I's mentorship, Ching Shih quickly learned the intricacies of maritime warfare, navigation, and piracy. She proved herself to be a capable and shrewd leader, earning the respect and loyalty of her fellow pirates through her strategic vision and fearless demeanor.

Wars

Ching Shih's rise to power came following the death of her husband, Cheng I, in 1807. With his passing, Ching Shih assumed command of the Red Flag Fleet, one of the most formidable pirate armadas in the South China Sea. Under her leadership, the Red Flag Fleet grew in strength and influence, dominating trade routes and coastal settlements throughout the region.

Ching Shih's pirate empire spanned hundreds of ships and tens of thousands of sailors, making her fleet the largest and most powerful in Chinese maritime history. She imposed a strict code of conduct on her followers, punishing disobedience and insubordination with severe penalties, including execution or flogging.

One of Ching Shih's most audacious acts came in 1809 when she challenged the might of the Qing Dynasty's navy in a series of daring raids along the Chinese coast. Despite facing overwhelming odds, Ching Shih's fleet emerged victorious, capturing numerous Qing warships and securing her dominance over the region.

Ching Shih's reign of terror continued for several years, as she plundered merchant vessels, extorted protection money from coastal villages, and evaded capture by imperial authorities. Her exploits made her a feared and respected figure throughout the South China Sea, earning her the nickname "The Terror of the South China Sea."

Death

Ching Shih's exact date of death is uncertain, but historical records suggest that she passed away in 1844 at the age of 69. Following her retirement from piracy, Ching Shih negotiated a pardon with the Qing government, allowing her to retire peacefully and live out her remaining years in obscurity.

Interesting Facts and Figures

- Ching Shih's pirate empire at its peak is estimated to have included over 1,500 ships and more than 80,000 sailors, making it one of the largest and most powerful naval forces in the world at the time.
- She implemented a strict code of conduct known as the "Articles of Ching Shih," which governed all aspects of pirate life, including division of loot, treatment of prisoners, and punishment for disobedience.
- Ching Shih's code of conduct included harsh penalties for offenses such as theft, desertion, or disobedience, but also provided protections for captured women and children, prohibiting rape or abuse.
- Despite her ruthless reputation, Ching Shih was known for her fairness and pragmatism, often negotiating peaceful resolutions with her enemies and avoiding unnecessary bloodshed whenever possible.
- Ching Shih's story has inspired numerous books, films, and television shows, cementing her legacy as one of the most legendary figures in pirate history.

Overall Win and Lose

Ching Shih's reign as the pirate queen of the South China Sea was marked by both triumphs and challenges. She amassed immense wealth and power, commanding the largest fleet in Chinese maritime history and striking fear into the hearts of sailors and coastal communities throughout the region.

Despite facing formidable adversaries, including the Qing Dynasty's navy and rival pirate factions, Ching Shih emerged victorious in many battles, securing her dominance over the South China Sea and amassing a fortune in plundered treasure.

However, Ching Shih's reign eventually came to an end with her decision to negotiate a pardon with the Qing government and retire from piracy. While she was able to live out her remaining years in peace, her decision to abandon her life of crime marked the end of an era of unparalleled piracy in Chinese history.

Nevertheless, Ching Shih's legacy as one of the most successful and feared pirates in history endures to this day, serving as a testament to her indomitable spirit, cunning leadership, and audacious feats of maritime warfare.

11

Crazy Horse (Lakota Sioux)

Crazy Horse, also known as Tasunke Witko in the Lakota language, stands as one of the most iconic and revered figures in Native American history. As a fearless warrior and leader of the Oglala Lakota Sioux, Crazy Horse played a significant role in resisting the encroachment of white settlers and the United States government onto Lakota lands during the turbulent period of the American Indian Wars. His unwavering dedication to his people's way of life and his legendary exploits in battle have immortalized him as a symbol of Native American resistance and resilience.

Birth

Crazy Horse was born around 1840 near present-day Rapid Creek, South Dakota, in the heart of Lakota territory. He was born into the Oglala band of the Lakota Sioux, a nomadic Plains Indian tribe known for their skilled horsemanship, hunting prowess, and warrior culture. From a young age, Crazy Horse was immersed in the traditions and customs of his people, learning the ways of the warrior and the importance of protecting his homeland and his people's way of life.

Early Life and Education

Growing up in the rugged landscape of the Great Plains, Crazy Horse received a traditional Lakota upbringing, learning the skills and knowledge necessary for survival in the harsh environment of the prairie. He honed his hunting and tracking skills, became proficient in horsemanship, and received instruction in the art of warfare from experienced warriors within his tribe.

From an early age, Crazy Horse exhibited exceptional courage, leadership, and a deep reverence for Lakota traditions and spirituality. He quickly distinguished himself as a natural leader among his peers, earning the respect and admiration of his fellow warriors through his bravery and integrity.

Wars

Crazy Horse's military career was defined by his leadership and participation in the resistance efforts against the encroachment of white settlers and the United States government onto Lakota lands. Throughout the 1860s and 1870s, he played a prominent role in various conflicts and battles between the Lakota Sioux and the U.S. Army, including the Dakota War of 1862, the Powder River War of 1865, and Red Cloud's War from 1866 to 1868.

One of Crazy Horse's most famous exploits came during Red Cloud's War, a conflict between the Lakota Sioux and the U.S. Army over control of the Bozeman Trail, a key supply route through Lakota territory. Crazy Horse distinguished himself as a brilliant tactician and strategist, leading daring raids against U.S. Army forts and supply convoys, including the legendary Fetterman Fight in December 1866, where he and his warriors ambushed and defeated a much larger U.S. Army force led by Captain William Fetterman.

Crazy Horse's greatest victory, however, came in June 1876 at the Battle of the Little Bighorn, also known as Custer's Last Stand. In this iconic battle, Crazy Horse, along with other Lakota leaders such as Sitting Bull and Gall, led a combined force of Lakota, Cheyenne, and Arapaho warriors in a stunning victory over Lieutenant Colonel George Armstrong Custer and the 7th Cavalry Regiment.

The Battle of the Little Bighorn, fought in present-day Montana, marked a decisive turning point in the Great Sioux War of 1876-77 and remains one of the most famous and studied battles in American military history. Crazy Horse's leadership and tactical brilliance played a crucial role in securing victory for the Lakota Sioux and dealing a devastating blow to U.S. military forces.

Death

Crazy Horse's life came to a tragic end on September 5, 1877, when he was fatally wounded during a confrontation with U.S. Army soldiers at Fort Robinson, Nebraska. The circumstances surrounding his death remain a subject of debate and controversy, with conflicting accounts of the events leading up to his demise.

According to some sources, Crazy Horse was killed while resisting arrest by U.S. authorities, while others claim that he was stabbed in the back by a soldier while being held in custody. Regardless of the specifics, Crazy Horse's death marked the end of an era of resistance and defiance among the Lakota Sioux and dealt a significant blow to their efforts to maintain their traditional way of life.

Interesting Facts and Figures

- Crazy Horse was renowned for his humility, courage, and unwavering commitment to his people's cause. He was known to shun material wealth and personal glory, instead focusing on protecting his homeland and preserving Lakota traditions and spirituality.
- He was a highly skilled and respected warrior, known for his exceptional horsemanship, marksmanship, and prowess in hand-to-hand combat. His battlefield exploits and leadership abilities earned him the admiration and respect of both allies and adversaries.
- Crazy Horse was deeply spiritual and believed in the importance of maintaining a strong connection to the natural world and the spirits of his ancestors. He often sought guidance through visions and dreams, which he interpreted as messages from the spirit world.
- Despite his legendary status, Crazy Horse left no known photographs or written records of his own. Most of what is known

about him comes from oral traditions, eyewitness accounts, and accounts written by others.
- Crazy Horse's legacy as a symbol of Native American resistance and resilience continues to resonate to this day, inspiring generations of Indigenous peoples and serving as a reminder of the ongoing struggles for land, sovereignty, and cultural survival.

Overall Win and Lose

Crazy Horse's legacy as a warrior and leader of the Lakota Sioux is defined by his unwavering commitment to defending his people's way of life and resisting the encroachment of white settlers and the U.S. government onto Lakota lands. Though he faced numerous challenges and setbacks throughout his life, including the loss of ancestral lands, displacement of his people, and ultimately his death at the hands of U.S. authorities, Crazy Horse's legacy endures as a symbol of Native American resistance and resilience.

While he may not have achieved a decisive victory in the conventional sense, Crazy Horse's courage, leadership, and determination inspired his people to continue fighting for their rights and sovereignty in the face of overwhelming odds. His legendary exploits in battle and his unwavering commitment to his people's cause have immortalized him as one of the most iconic figures in Native American history, leaving an indelible mark on the collective consciousness of Indigenous peoples and serving as a source of inspiration for generations to come.

12

El Cid (Spain)

Rodrigo Díaz de Vivar, commonly known as El Cid, is a legendary figure in Spanish history, celebrated as one of the greatest warriors and military leaders of the medieval period. Born into the noble class of medieval Spain, El Cid rose to prominence during the era of the Reconquista, the centuries-long struggle to reconquer the Iberian Peninsula from Moorish rule. His remarkable military exploits, unwavering loyalty to his Christian faith, and complex political maneuvering have immortalized him as a symbol of valor, chivalry, and national identity in Spain.

Birth

El Cid, born Rodrigo Díaz de Vivar, was born in 1043 in the town of Vivar del Cid, near Burgos, in the Kingdom of Castile, which is now part of northern Spain. He was born into a noble family of minor nobility, with his father Diego Lainez holding the position of minor noble and his mother Teresa Rodríguez being of the higher nobility.

Early Life and Education

Little is known about El Cid's early life and education, but it is believed that he received training in the arts of warfare, horsemanship, and chivalry from a young age, as was customary for noble youths of his time. He likely participated in knightly tournaments and military exercises, honing his skills as a warrior and leader.

At the age of fourteen, El Cid fought alongside his father in the service of King Ferdinand I of Castile, gaining valuable experience in combat and earning a reputation for bravery and martial prowess. His early experiences on the battlefield would shape his future as a military leader and hero of the Reconquista.

Wars

El Cid's military career was characterized by his service to various Christian kingdoms in the Iberian Peninsula during the Reconquista, a period of intense conflict between Christian and Muslim forces for control of Spain. Throughout his life, El Cid fought in numerous battles and campaigns, earning fame and renown as a formidable warrior and tactician.

One of El Cid's most famous campaigns came in 1067 when he led an expedition against the Moorish kingdom of Zaragoza, which had rebelled against the Christian king of Aragon. El Cid's forces besieged the city for several months before capturing it and restoring it to Christian rule. His success in this campaign earned him the favor of King Sancho II of Castile and established his reputation as a skilled military commander.

In 1072, El Cid fell out of favor with King Alfonso VI of Castile and was exiled from the kingdom. Undeterred, he offered his services to the Moorish king of Zaragoza, Yusuf al-Mu'tamin, and fought alongside Muslim forces against Christian armies in the ongoing conflicts of the Reconquista. Despite his alliance with the Moors, El Cid remained a devout Christian and continued to uphold his faith throughout his military campaigns.

In 1087, El Cid achieved his most significant victory when he captured the city of Valencia from Moorish control after a lengthy siege. The conquest of Valencia established El Cid as a powerful ruler in his own right and solidified his reputation as a hero of the Reconquista. He ruled Valencia as an independent lord until he died in 1099, consolidating his power and expanding his territory in the region.

Death

El Cid died in Valencia on July 10, 1099, at the age of fifty-six. His death marked the end of an era in Spanish history and left a void in the struggle against Moorish rule in the Iberian Peninsula. Despite his passing, El Cid's legacy lived on, inspiring future generations of Spaniards to continue the fight for Christian supremacy in Spain and shaping the course of medieval history in the region.

Interesting Facts and Figures

- El Cid's nickname, "El Cid," is derived from the Arabic term "Sayyid," meaning "lord" or "master." It was bestowed upon him by the Moors in recognition of his leadership and valor on the battlefield.
- El Cid is celebrated as a national hero in Spain, revered for his courage, honor, and loyalty to his Christian faith and his country. His exploits have been immortalized in numerous works of literature, art, and film, cementing his status as a legendary figure in Spanish history.
- El Cid's sword, known as "Tizona," is one of the most famous weapons in Spanish history. According to legend, it was forged by Moorish craftsmen and possessed magical powers that made it unbeatable in battle. Tizona is now housed in the Museum of Burgos in Spain.
- Despite his reputation as a fearless warrior, El Cid was also known for his chivalry and generosity towards his enemies. He was renowned for sparing the lives of defeated foes and treating prisoners with dignity and respect, earning him the admiration of both friends and foes alike.
- El Cid's military campaigns played a crucial role in the eventual reconquest of Spain by Christian forces, paving the way for the establishment of the Kingdom of Castile and the eventual unification of Spain under Christian rule.

Overall Win and Lose

El Cid's military career was marked by both triumphs and challenges, victories and setbacks. While he achieved remarkable success in battle and established himself as a legendary figure in Spanish history, he also faced personal and political obstacles that tested his resolve and loyalty.

Despite his exile from Castile and his alliance with Moorish rulers, El Cid remained steadfast in his commitment to his Christian faith and his country. His conquest of Valencia and his efforts to resist Moorish rule in the Iberian Peninsula contributed significantly to the eventual reconquest of Spain by Christian forces and the establishment of a unified Christian kingdom.

In the end, El Cid's legacy as a hero of the Reconquista endures as a symbol of valor, honor, and national identity in Spain. His life and achievements continue to inspire admiration and reverence among Spaniards and people around the world, ensuring that the memory of El Cid will live on for generations to come.

13

Erwin Rommel (Germany)

Field Marshal Erwin Rommel, also known as the "Desert Fox," was one of Germany's most respected and renowned military commanders during World War II. His strategic brilliance, tactical innovation, and charismatic leadership earned him a formidable reputation on both sides of the conflict. Rommel's military career spanned two world wars, and his legacy continues to fascinate historians and military enthusiasts alike.

Birth

Erwin Johannes Eugen Rommel was born on November 15, 1891, in Heidenheim an der Brenz, in the Kingdom of Württemberg, part of the German Empire. He was the third of five children born to Erwin Rommel Sr., a schoolmaster and later a headmaster, and Helene von Lutz, a daughter of a local government official. From an early age, Rommel showed a keen interest in military history and strategy, foreshadowing his future career as a military leader.

Early Life and Education

Rommel attended school in his hometown and later the Realgymnasium in Ulm. After completing his education, he joined the local 124th Infantry Regiment as an officer cadet in 1910. His military training instilled in him a sense of discipline, duty, and devotion to his country, values that would shape his character and define his career as a soldier.

Wars

Rommel's military career began during World War I when he served as a lieutenant in the German Army on the Western Front. He distinguished himself as a brave and resourceful leader, earning several awards for valor, including the Iron Cross, Second Class, and the Iron Cross, First Class.

After the war, Rommel remained in the military and held various staff and instructional positions in the interwar period. He also wrote several influential books on military tactics and strategy, including "Infanterie Greift An" ("Infantry Attacks"), which became a standard textbook for infantry officers in Germany and other countries.

Rommel's meteoric rise to fame came during World War II when he commanded the 7th Panzer Division during the invasion of France in 1940. His innovative tactics, rapid maneuvering, and bold leadership played a crucial role in the stunning success of the German Blitzkrieg (lightning war) strategy, which resulted in the rapid defeat of France and the Low Countries.

Rommel's reputation as a brilliant military strategist was further enhanced during his command of the Afrika Korps in North Africa. His tactical genius and aggressive leadership earned him the nickname "the Desert Fox" and made him a formidable adversary for Allied forces in the North African campaign.

Despite being outnumbered and outgunned, Rommel's forces achieved a series of stunning victories against British and Commonwealth troops, including the capture of Tobruk in 1942. His successes in North Africa made him a national hero in Germany and earned him the admiration of his enemies.

However, Rommel's fortunes began to decline following the Allied landings in North Africa and the subsequent defeat of Axis forces at the Battle of El Alamein in late 1942. Despite his tactical brilliance, Rommel's supply lines were stretched thin, and he was unable to withstand the combined strength of Allied forces in North Africa.

Following his defeat in North Africa, Rommel was reassigned to command Army Group B in France, where he was tasked with fortifying the Atlantic Wall in anticipation of an Allied invasion. Despite his best efforts, he was unable to prevent the successful Allied landings in Normandy on D-Day, June 6, 1944.

Death

Rommel's involvement in the July 20, 1944, plot to assassinate Adolf Hitler sealed his fate. Although Rommel was not directly involved in the conspiracy, his close association with the conspirators led to his implication in the plot. Faced with the choice of standing trial and risking the safety of his family or taking his own life, Rommel chose the latter.

On October 14, 1944, Rommel was visited at his home by two officers from the Nazi regime. They presented him with an ultimatum: either stand trial for his involvement in the plot to assassinate Hitler or take his own life and be given a state funeral with full military honors. Rommel chose the latter option and ingested a cyanide capsule, ending his life at the age of 52.

Interesting Facts and Figures

- Rommel was known for his chivalrous conduct on the battlefield and his concern for the welfare of his troops. He was deeply respected by both his subordinates and his enemies for his integrity, courage, and professionalism.
- Rommel was one of the few German commanders to openly criticize Nazi atrocities, including the treatment of prisoners of war and civilians. Despite his loyalty to the German military, he opposed the excesses of the Nazi regime and sought to distance himself from its crimes.
- Rommel's leadership style emphasized decentralized command, initiative, and flexibility, allowing his subordinates to adapt to changing battlefield conditions and take advantage of enemy weaknesses.
- Rommel's military successes in North Africa made him a popular figure in Germany and a symbol of hope for the German people during the darkest days of the war. His reputation as a brilliant

military strategist and charismatic leader earned him widespread admiration and respect both at home and abroad.

Overall Win and Lose

Erwin Rommel's military career was marked by both triumphs and setbacks, victories and defeats. While he achieved remarkable success on the battlefield and earned a reputation as one of the most talented and respected military commanders of his time, he was ultimately unable to overcome the combined strength of the Allied forces.

Rommel's tactical brilliance and innovative leadership played a crucial role in many of the German Army's most significant victories during World War II, including the conquest of France and the early successes in North Africa. However, his inability to secure victory in the decisive battles of El Alamein and Normandy sealed the fate of Axis forces in North Africa and Western Europe.

Despite his military prowess, Rommel's involvement in the July 20 plot against Hitler tarnished his legacy and led to his untimely death. His decision to take his own life rather than face trial for his alleged involvement in the conspiracy remains a subject of debate and controversy among historians and scholars.

Nevertheless, Rommel's contributions to military theory and strategy continue to be studied and admired by military professionals around the world. His emphasis on decentralized command, flexibility, and initiative remains relevant in modern warfare, ensuring that his legacy as the "Desert Fox" will endure for generations to come.

14

Frederick the Great (Prussia)

Frederick II, commonly known as Frederick the Great, was a pivotal figure in European history and one of the most renowned monarchs of the 18th century. As the King of Prussia from 1740 to 1786, Frederick transformed his small and fragmented kingdom into a major European power through his military prowess, administrative reforms, and patronage of the arts and culture. His reign marked a period of significant political, social, and cultural development in Prussia and left a lasting impact on the course of European history.

Birth

Frederick was born on January 24, 1712, in Berlin, the capital of the Kingdom of Prussia, to Frederick William I, Elector of Brandenburg, and Sophia Dorothea of Hanover. From a young age, Frederick showed an aptitude for intellectual pursuits and military matters, much to the dismay of his stern and authoritarian father, who favored a strict military upbringing for his son.

Early Life and Education

Despite his father's wishes, Frederick received a humanist education, studying literature, philosophy, and the arts under private tutors. He developed a lifelong passion for the works of classical authors such as Voltaire and Cicero, which would later influence his intellectual and cultural pursuits as king.

At the age of 18, Frederick was compelled to join the Prussian Army under his father's strict military regime. His relationship with his father was strained, and Frederick often chafed under the rigid discipline of military life. However, his experiences in the army would shape his character and provide him with valuable insights into military strategy and leadership.

Wars

Frederick's military career began in earnest with the outbreak of the War of the Austrian Succession in 1740, following the death of Emperor Charles VI of Austria. As the ruler of Prussia, Frederick seized the opportunity to assert his territorial ambitions and launched an invasion of the Austrian province of Silesia, igniting the first of many conflicts that would define his reign.

Despite being outnumbered and facing formidable enemies, Frederick's tactical brilliance and audacity on the battlefield allowed him to achieve a series of stunning victories against Austrian and Allied forces. His military successes in Silesia earned him the admiration of his contemporaries and established Prussia as a major power in Central Europe.

One of Frederick's most famous campaigns came during the Seven Years' War (1756-1763), a continent-wide conflict that pitted Prussia against an alliance of European powers led by Austria, France, and Russia. Despite being surrounded by enemies on all sides, Frederick managed to stave off multiple invasions and defend Prussian territory through a combination of strategic maneuvering, decisive battles, and diplomatic alliances.

Frederick's military genius was evident in battles such as Rossbach (1757) and Leuthen (1757), where he achieved decisive victories against numerically superior opponents. His tactical innovations, including rapid infantry movements and flexible formations, revolutionized warfare and earned him a reputation as one of the greatest military commanders of his time.

Despite his military successes, the Seven Years' War took a heavy toll on Prussia, both economically and territorially. By the war's end, Prussia had lost significant territories and suffered extensive damage to its economy and infrastructure. However, Frederick's resilience and determination ensured that Prussia emerged from the conflict with its sovereignty intact, albeit weakened.

Death

Frederick the Great died on August 17, 1786, at the age of 74, at his beloved palace of Sanssouci in Potsdam, near Berlin. His death marked the end of an era in Prussian history and left a void in European politics and culture. Frederick was succeeded by his nephew, Frederick William II, who continued his policies of reform and modernization.

Interesting Facts and Figures

- Frederick the Great was a prolific patron of the arts and culture, fostering the development of literature, music, and philosophy in Prussia. He maintained a close correspondence with the French philosopher Voltaire and invited him to reside at his court in Potsdam, where he enjoyed intellectual discussions and debates.
- Frederick was an accomplished musician and composer, known for his skill on the flute and his patronage of the arts. He composed over 100 flute sonatas, concertos, and symphonies, which are still performed and admired today.
- Frederick's reign saw significant advances in education, infrastructure, and administration in Prussia. He implemented reforms to modernize the Prussian bureaucracy, improve the efficiency of government, and promote economic development.
- Frederick's military reforms transformed the Prussian Army into one of the most disciplined and effective fighting forces in Europe. He introduced standardized training, improved logistics, and streamlined command structures, laying the foundation for Prussia's future military successes.

- Frederick's reign saw the expansion of Prussia's territorial holdings through a combination of conquest, diplomacy, and inheritance. By the end of his reign, Prussia had become a major European power, rivaling traditional great powers such as Austria, France, and Russia.

Overall Win and Lose

Frederick the Great's reign was marked by both triumphs and challenges, victories and defeats. While he achieved remarkable success in expanding Prussia's territory, modernizing its administration, and reforming its military, he also faced significant obstacles and setbacks along the way.

Despite his military genius and diplomatic skill, Frederick's aggressive territorial ambitions and confrontational approach to foreign policy often led to conflicts with Prussia's neighbors and strained relations with other European powers. The Seven Years' War, in particular, tested Prussia's resilience and resources to the limit, resulting in heavy casualties and territorial losses.

However, Frederick's legacy as a visionary leader, military genius, and patron of the arts endures to this day. His reforms laid the foundation for Prussia's future greatness and contributed to the rise of Germany as a unified and powerful nation in the 19th century. Frederick's achievements continue to be celebrated in Germany and around the world, cementing his place as one of the most influential figures in European.

15

Genghis Khan (Mongolia)

Genghis Khan, born in Temüjin, is one of history's most iconic and formidable conquerors. Rising from humble beginnings on the Mongolian steppes, he forged the largest contiguous land empire in history, stretching from Eastern Europe to the Pacific Ocean. His military genius, strategic vision, and administrative reforms transformed the world and left an indelible mark on human history. Despite his reputation as a ruthless warrior, Genghis Khan's legacy also includes significant contributions to trade, culture, and governance.

Birth

Temüjin, later known as Genghis Khan, was born in 1162 near the Onon River in present-day Mongolia. His father, Yesügei, was the leader of the Borjigin tribe, and his mother, Hoelun, was from the Olkhonud tribe. Temüjin's early life was marked by hardship and adversity, as his father was poisoned by rival tribes when Temüjin was only nine years old, leaving his family vulnerable and destitute.

Early Life and Education

As a young boy, Temüjin endured the harsh conditions of nomadic life on the Mongolian steppes. He learned essential survival skills such as hunting, horseback riding, and combat from his family and the other members of his tribe. Despite his humble beginnings, Temüjin exhibited exceptional leadership qualities and a keen intellect from an early age.

At the age of nine, Temüjin was betrothed to Börte, a union arranged by his father to strengthen alliances between their tribes. The marriage would prove to be a significant factor in Temüjin's rise to power, as Börte's family provided crucial support during his early struggles for supremacy.

Wars

Temüjin's path to power was fraught with challenges and conflicts as he navigated the complex politics of the Mongolian steppe. In the absence of strong central authority, rival clans and tribes vied for dominance, leading to frequent skirmishes and battles.

Temüjin's rise to power began in earnest in 1186 when he was elected as the Khan of the Mongols, following a series of successful military campaigns against rival clans. As Khan, Temüjin sought to consolidate his authority and unite the disparate Mongol tribes under his leadership. He implemented a series of administrative and military reforms to strengthen his position and expand his influence.

One of Temüjin's most significant military achievements came in 1206 when he convened a grand assembly of Mongol chieftains and tribal leaders, where he was proclaimed Genghis Khan, or "Universal Ruler," of all Mongols. This marked the beginning of the Mongol Empire, which would go on to become the largest land empire in history.

Under Genghis Khan's leadership, the Mongol Empire embarked on a relentless campaign of conquest, expanding its territory through a combination of military prowess, strategic cunning, and psychological warfare. Genghis Khan's military strategy was characterized by speed, mobility, and coordination, allowing his forces to overcome much larger and more established empires.

One of Genghis Khan's most famous conquests came in 1215 when his armies captured the Jin Dynasty's capital of Zhongdu (present-day Beijing), marking the beginning of Mongol rule in China. Over the next decade, the Mongols would conquer much of northern China, paving the way for the establishment of the Yuan Dynasty under Genghis Khan's grandson, Kublai Khan.

Genghis Khan's military campaigns extended far beyond the borders of China, encompassing vast swathes of Central Asia, the Middle East, and Eastern Europe. His armies sacked cities, razed fortresses, and defeated countless enemies, leaving a trail of destruction and devastation in their wake.

Death

Genghis Khan died in 1227 at the age of approximately 65, while leading a military campaign against the Western Xia Dynasty in present-day China. The exact cause of his death remains uncertain, with some accounts suggesting that he was killed in battle, while others claim that he succumbed to illness or injury.

Following his death, Genghis Khan was buried in an unmarked grave by Mongol tradition, and the location of his tomb remains a mystery to this day. Despite his passing, Genghis Khan's legacy lived on through his descendants and the vast empire he had forged.

Interesting Facts and Figures

- Genghis Khan's military conquests resulted in the deaths of millions of people and the displacement of countless others. However, his empire also facilitated trade, cultural exchange, and technological innovation, leading to the emergence of the Pax Mongolica, or "Mongol Peace," a period of relative stability and prosperity in Eurasia.
- Genghis Khan was known for his tolerance of different religions and cultures, allowing freedom of worship and granting autonomy to conquered peoples who submitted to Mongol rule. He encouraged religious diversity and appointed members of various ethnic and religious groups to positions of authority within his empire.
- Genghis Khan was a shrewd diplomat and negotiator, using both military force and diplomacy to expand his empire and secure alliances with neighboring states. He employed a network of spies and envoys to gather intelligence and maintain communication

with distant territories, allowing him to govern his vast empire effectively.
- Genghis Khan's legacy extends beyond his military conquests to include significant contributions to law, governance, and administration. He codified Mongol customary law, established a system of tribute and taxation, and implemented reforms to promote trade, agriculture, and infrastructure development.
- Genghis Khan's influence continues to be felt in modern-day Mongolia and throughout the world, where he is revered as a national hero and a symbol of Mongolian identity and pride. His legacy as a visionary leader, military genius, and founder of one of history's greatest empires endures to this day.

Overall Win and Lose

Genghis Khan's legacy is complex and multifaceted, encompassing both triumphs and tragedies. While his military conquests brought about unparalleled destruction and suffering, they also laid the foundation for centuries of cultural exchange, economic prosperity, and technological advancement.

Despite his ruthless reputation as a conqueror, Genghis Khan's achievements as a statesman, lawmaker, and visionary leader cannot be overlooked. His empire paved the way for the unification of Eurasia and the emergence of a new era of global interconnectedness.

In the grand sweep of history, Genghis Khan's legacy is a testament to the enduring power of human ambition, resilience, and innovation. His impact on the world continues to be felt to this day, reminding us of the complexities of conquest, empire-building, and the human experience.

16

Geronimo (Apache)

Geronimo, whose Apache name was Goyaałé, was a prominent leader and warrior of the Chiricahua Apache tribe, known for his fierce resistance against Mexican and American expansion into Apache territories in the southwestern United States. He became a symbol of Native American resistance and defiance against encroaching settlers and government policies that sought to displace and subjugate Indigenous peoples. Geronimo's life is a testament to the struggle for freedom and self-determination in the face of overwhelming odds.

Birth

Geronimo was born in 1829 near the headwaters of the Gila River in what is now modern-day New Mexico. He was born into the Bedonkohe band of the Chiricahua Apache tribe, a group known for their warrior tradition and fierce independence. From a young age, Geronimo was raised in the traditions of his people, learning the skills of hunting, tracking, and warfare that would later define his life.

Early Life and Education

As a young boy, Geronimo experienced the upheaval caused by the encroachment of white settlers and the increasing presence of Mexican and American military forces in Apache territory. He witnessed firsthand the displacement of his people from their ancestral lands and the erosion of their traditional way of life. These experiences would shape

Geronimo's worldview and fuel his determination to resist outside forces seeking to control Apache lands.

Geronimo received his education in the ways of the Apache from his family and tribal elders, who taught him the customs, traditions, and oral history of his people. He also learned the art of warfare, becoming skilled in the use of weapons such as bows, arrows, and spears, as well as tactics such as ambushes and guerrilla warfare.

Wars

Geronimo's life was defined by conflict and resistance against Mexican and American forces seeking to assert control over Apache lands. Throughout his adult life, he led numerous raids and skirmishes against settlers, miners, and soldiers, earning a reputation as a fearless and relentless warrior.

One of Geronimo's earliest military engagements came in the 1850s during the Apache Wars, a series of conflicts between Apache tribes and Mexican and American forces. Geronimo distinguished himself as a fierce and resourceful leader, leading his band of warriors in daring raids and ambushes against enemy encampments and settlements.

Geronimo's most famous campaign came in the late 1870s and early 1880s when he led a series of raids across the southwestern United States, eluding capture by Mexican and American troops for over a decade. During this time, Geronimo became a legendary figure among both Native Americans and white settlers, admired for his bravery, cunning, and tenacity.

In 1886, Geronimo surrendered to American forces after years of evading capture. His surrender marked the end of the Apache Wars and the beginning of a new chapter in Geronimo's life as a prisoner of war. He and his band were sent to live in exile in Florida before being transferred to reservations in Oklahoma and later, in 1894, to Fort Sill in present-day Oklahoma.

Despite his captivity, Geronimo continued to resist assimilation and advocate for the rights of his people. He traveled extensively, speaking out against government policies that sought to undermine Apache sovereignty and culture. In 1905, he published his autobiography, "Geronimo: His Own Story," which offered a firsthand account of his life and experiences as a warrior and leader.

Death

Geronimo died on February 17, 1909, at Fort Sill, Oklahoma, at the age of approximately 79. He was buried in the Apache Cemetery at Fort Sill, where his gravesite remains a place of pilgrimage and reverence for Native Americans and others inspired by his legacy of resistance and resilience.

Interesting Facts and Figures

- Geronimo's name has become synonymous with courage and defiance. The battle cry "Geronimo!" is said to have originated during his raids against Mexican and American forces, as his enemies would shout his name in fear and alarm when he and his warriors attacked.
- Despite his reputation as a fearsome warrior, Geronimo was also known for his compassion and kindness towards his people. He was a respected leader and healer within the Apache community, known for his wisdom and generosity.
- Geronimo's surrender in 1886 marked the end of armed resistance by the Apache tribes against American forces. However, his legacy as a symbol of Native American resistance and resilience continues to inspire Indigenous peoples and others fighting for justice and equality.
- Geronimo's image and likeness have been used in popular culture, literature, and media to romanticize and mythologize the American West. However, his true story is one of struggle, sacrifice, and survival in the face of overwhelming odds.

Overall Win and Lose

Geronimo's life was marked by both triumphs and tragedies, victories and defeats. While he achieved legendary status as a warrior and leader of his people, he also experienced the loss of his homeland, the displacement of his people, and the erosion of their traditional way of life.

In the broader context of American history, Geronimo's resistance against encroaching settlers and government policies represented a larger struggle for Indigenous rights, sovereignty, and self-determination. While he ultimately surrendered to American forces, his legacy as a symbol of Native American resistance and resilience endures to this day, inspiring future generations to continue the fight for justice and equality.

17

Hannibal Barca (Carthag)

Hannibal Barca, the Carthaginian general and military strategist, stands as one of history's greatest military commanders. Born into a prominent Carthaginian family, Hannibal rose to prominence during the Second Punic War, where he led Carthage's armies against the formidable Roman Republic. His daring tactics, innovative strategies, and legendary crossing of the Alps with elephants have solidified his place in military history. Hannibal's campaigns against Rome are celebrated for their audacity, and his legacy continues to inspire military leaders and historians alike.

Birth

Hannibal Barca was born in 247 BCE in the city of Carthage, located in present-day Tunisia. He was born into the Barcid family, one of the leading noble families of Carthage, renowned for their military prowess and leadership. Hannibal's father, Hamilcar Barca, was a distinguished Carthaginian general who instilled in his son a deep sense of loyalty to Carthage and a burning desire to avenge its defeat in the First Punic War.

Early Life and Education

Hannibal grew up surrounded by the tumult of Carthaginian politics and the looming threat of Roman expansionism. From a young age, he was immersed in the art of war, accompanying his father on military campaigns and witnessing firsthand the brutality of conflict. Under his father's tutelage, Hannibal developed a keen understanding of military strategy and tactics, as well as a fierce determination to challenge Rome's hegemony in the Mediterranean.

Hannibal's education extended beyond the battlefield to include lessons in diplomacy, statesmanship, and administration. He was well-versed in the history and traditions of Carthage, as well as the cultures and customs of its allies and enemies. These early experiences would shape Hannibal's worldview and inform his later actions as a military leader.

Wars

Hannibal's military career began in earnest during the Second Punic War (218-201 BCE), a conflict between Carthage and Rome for control of the western Mediterranean. In 218 BCE, Hannibal launched a daring invasion of Italy, leading his army and a contingent of war elephants across the Alps from Spain into Roman territory. The crossing of the Alps remains one of the most audacious feats in military history and is a testament to Hannibal's strategic genius and determination.

Once in Italy, Hannibal won a series of stunning victories against Roman forces, including the battles of Trebia (218 BCE), Lake Trasimene (217 BCE), and Cannae (216 BCE). His tactics, which emphasized mobility, surprise, and the exploitation of enemy weaknesses, confounded and demoralized the Romans, who had never faced an adversary of Hannibal's caliber.

Despite his early successes, Hannibal's campaign in Italy ultimately faltered due to a lack of reinforcements and support from Carthage. The Roman strategy of attrition and the refusal to engage Hannibal in open battle gradually wore down his forces and forced him to retreat to southern Italy. Despite several attempts to negotiate peace with Rome, Hannibal was unable to secure a favorable settlement, and the war dragged on for years.

In 203 BCE, Hannibal returned to Carthage to defend the city against a Roman invasion led by Scipio Africanus. The decisive battle of the war took place at Zama in 202 BCE, where Hannibal's forces were defeated by Scipio's army, effectively ending Carthage's hopes of victory. The subsequent Treaty of Zama imposed harsh terms on Carthage, including heavy reparations, territorial concessions, and restrictions on its military capabilities.

Death

After the defeat at Zama, Hannibal's political fortunes in Carthage waned, and he went into exile to escape the vengeance of his enemies. He spent the remaining years of his life traveling throughout the Mediterranean, seeking refuge in various kingdoms and city-states. In 183 or 181 BCE, facing capture by the Romans, Hannibal chose to take his own life rather than surrender to his enemies. He died at the age of approximately 64, a broken but still revered figure among his people.

Interesting Facts and Figures

- Hannibal's crossing of the Alps with war elephants is one of the most celebrated military maneuvers in history. Despite the treacherous terrain, harsh weather, and hostile tribes, Hannibal managed to lead his army, including a contingent of elephants, through the mountain passes and into Italy, catching the Romans off guard and securing a foothold in their territory.
- Hannibal's victory at the Battle of Cannae in 216 BCE is considered one of the greatest tactical triumphs in military history. Despite being outnumbered nearly two to one, Hannibal's innovative use of flanking maneuvers and cavalry charges resulted in a devastating defeat for the Roman army, with an estimated 50,000 Roman soldiers killed or captured.
- Hannibal's military campaigns in Italy inspired fear and admiration among his enemies, who regarded him as a formidable and cunning adversary. His ability to outmaneuver and outwit the Romans earned him a reputation as one of the greatest military commanders of his time, and his tactics continue to be studied and admired by military historians and strategists.

- Despite his defeat in the Second Punic War, Hannibal's legacy endured in Carthage and beyond. He became a symbol of resistance against foreign domination and a rallying point for those who sought to challenge Rome's hegemony in the Mediterranean. His name became synonymous with courage, determination, and defiance, inspiring future generations of leaders and revolutionaries.
- Hannibal's life and legacy have been the subject of numerous books, films, and works of art, cementing his place as one of the most iconic figures in military history. His story continues to captivate the imagination of people around the world, serving as a reminder of the power of leadership, strategy, and perseverance in the face of adversity.

Overall Win and Lose

Hannibal Barca's military career was marked by both triumphs and setbacks, victories and defeats. While he achieved stunning successes against Rome in Italy, including the legendary victories at Trebia, Lake Trasimene, and Cannae, he ultimately failed to secure a decisive victory that would have forced Rome to sue for peace on favorable terms.

Despite his defeat in the Second Punic War, Hannibal's legacy endures as one of the greatest military commanders in history. His daring tactics, innovative strategies, and legendary crossing of the Alps continue to inspire awe and admiration, cementing his place in the annals of military history. While Hannibal may have lost the war against Rome, his indomitable spirit and enduring legacy ensure that he will be remembered as a symbol of courage, determination, and defiance for generations to come.

18

Harald Hardrada (Norway)

Harald Sigurdsson, famously known as Harald Hardrada, was a Norwegian king and a formidable warrior who played a significant role in the tumultuous political landscape of 11th-century Scandinavia and Europe. Harald's life was marked by his military exploits, ambition for power, and relentless pursuit of glory. He is remembered as one of the last great Viking kings and his attempt to conquer England in 1066 is one of the most iconic events of the Viking Age.

Birth

Harald Hardrada was born in 1015 in Ringerike, Norway, into a noble family of Viking warriors. His father, Sigurd Syr, was a chieftain of significant influence in the region. Harald's upbringing was steeped in the traditions of Norse culture, where martial prowess and honor held paramount importance. From an early age, Harald displayed exceptional skill in combat and leadership, foreshadowing his future as a formidable warrior and ruler.

Early Life and Education

Harald's early years were marked by political upheaval and conflict as rival chieftains vied for power in Norway. At the age of fifteen, Harald participated in his first battle alongside his half-brother, King Olaf II of Norway, also known as Saint Olaf. Harald quickly gained a reputation for bravery and tactical acumen, distinguishing himself in numerous battles against rival claimants to the Norwegian throne.

Despite his youth, Harald's military prowess and charisma soon earned him the loyalty and support of his fellow warriors. He quickly rose through the ranks of the Norwegian nobility, forging alliances and consolidating his power base through strategic marriages and political maneuvering.

Wars

Harald's military career reached its zenith during the tumultuous period known as the Norwegian Civil War (1130-1240), a protracted struggle for control of the Norwegian throne between rival factions of the Norwegian aristocracy. Harald emerged as a key player in this conflict, leading his forces in a series of bloody battles and sieges against his rivals.

In 1046, Harald's half-brother, Magnus the Good, became the sole ruler of Norway after a period of uneasy co-rule. Harald served as Magnus's trusted lieutenant and commander of the Norwegian army, leading successful campaigns against rebellious nobles and external threats. However, tensions between the two brothers simmered beneath the surface, fueled by ambition and rivalry.

Following Magnus's death in 1047, Harald seized the opportunity to assert his claim to the Norwegian throne, igniting a new phase of conflict and instability. He faced fierce opposition from Magnus's supporters, as well as rival claimants to the throne, including Magnus's illegitimate son, Harald Sigurdsson (later known as Harald Hardrada).

Harald's quest for power and glory extended beyond the borders of Norway, as he sought to expand his influence and territories through conquest and plunder. In 1066, Harald embarked on his most ambitious campaign yet: the invasion of England.

Invasion of England:

In 1066, Harald Hardrada set sail for England with a formidable fleet and army, intent on seizing the English throne from King Harold Godwinson. Harald's invasion force landed in northern England, where they quickly defeated the local Anglo-Saxon forces at the Battle of Fulford on September 20, 1066.

Flushed with victory, Harald marched southward to challenge King Harold's army, which had hurriedly marched north to confront the Norwegian invaders. On September 25, 1066, the two armies clashed at the Battle of Stamford Bridge, near the town of York.

Despite being heavily outnumbered, Harald's forces initially held the upper hand, inflicting heavy casualties on the Anglo-Saxon army. However, the tide of battle turned when King Harold's reinforcements arrived, catching Harald's army by surprise and turning the tide of battle in favor of the English.

In the ensuing chaos, Harald Hardrada was struck by an arrow and mortally wounded. His death marked the end of the Viking Age and the final chapter in the saga of Norse expansion into England. Harald's defeat at Stamford Bridge paved the way for the Norman Conquest of England by William the Conqueror just a few weeks later.

Death

Harald Hardrada died on September 25, 1066, at the Battle of Stamford Bridge, at the age of 51. His death marked the end of an era in Norwegian and Scandinavian history and paved the way for significant political and cultural changes in the region.

Interesting Facts and Figures

- Harald Hardrada's epithet, "Hardrada," means "hard ruler" or "stern councilor" in Old Norse, reflecting his reputation as a strong and uncompromising leader.
- Harald was renowned for his exceptional physical strength and martial prowess. He was said to be unusually tall and strong, with a fearsome presence on the battlefield.
- Harald Hardrada's invasion of England in 1066 was one of the largest Viking military expeditions ever mounted. His fleet consisted of over 300 ships and an estimated 9,000 soldiers, including experienced warriors and mercenaries from across Scandinavia.
- Despite his defeat at Stamford Bridge, Harald Hardrada's legacy endured in Norway and beyond. He is remembered as one of

Norway's greatest kings and a symbol of Viking valor and martial prowess.
- Harald Hardrada's life and exploits have been immortalized in Norse sagas, medieval chronicles, and later works of literature and art. His legacy continues to capture the imagination of people around the world, serving as a reminder of the Viking Age and its lasting impact on European history.

Overall Win and Lose

Harald Hardrada's life was characterized by ambition, adventure, and conflict. While he achieved considerable success as a military leader and ruler of Norway, his quest for power ultimately ended in defeat at the Battle of Stamford Bridge. Despite this setback, Harald's legacy as one of the last great Viking kings endures, immortalized in sagas, songs, and legends that celebrate his courage, leadership, and indomitable spirit.

19

Hattori Hanzo (Japan)

Hattori Hanzo, also known as Hattori Masanari, was a legendary samurai and ninja who rose to prominence during Japan's Sengoku period (1467-1603), a time of intense civil strife and warfare. Hanzo's exceptional skills as a warrior, tactician, and strategist earned him a place among the most revered figures in Japanese history. He is best remembered for his service to the Tokugawa clan, particularly his role in the rise to power of Tokugawa Ieyasu, the founder of the Tokugawa shogunate. Hattori Hanzo's legacy as a master of espionage and covert operations continues to inspire admiration and fascination to this day.

Birth

Hattori Hanzo was born in 1542 in the province of Mikawa, in what is now modern-day Aichi Prefecture, Japan. He was born into a prestigious samurai family with a long tradition of military service to the Tokugawa clan. From a young age, Hanzo demonstrated exceptional martial skills and an aptitude for strategy, setting him on the path to becoming one of Japan's most renowned warriors.

Early Life and Education

Hattori Hanzo received rigorous training in martial arts and warfare from a young age, honing his skills in swordsmanship, archery, horsemanship, and hand-to-hand combat. He studied under renowned masters of the martial arts, learning both traditional samurai techniques and the secretive arts of ninjutsu, or ninja warfare.

Hanzo's education extended beyond the battlefield to include lessons in tactics, strategy, and military leadership. He studied the strategies of ancient Chinese military texts such as Sun Tzu's "The Art of War," as well as Japanese works on military strategy and philosophy.

Wars

Hattori Hanzo's military career coincided with one of the most turbulent periods in Japanese history, as rival warlords and daimyo vied for control of Japan. Hanzo first rose to prominence as a retainer of Tokugawa Ieyasu, who would later become one of the most powerful figures in Japanese history.

During the Battle of Mikatagahara in 1573, Hattori Hanzo distinguished himself as a fearless and skilled warrior, leading a contingent of samurai in a decisive charge against enemy forces. His valor and tactical acumen earned him the respect and admiration of his fellow warriors and the attention of Tokugawa Ieyasu, who recognized Hanzo's potential as a valuable ally.

Throughout the Sengoku period, Hanzo served as a trusted advisor and military commander in Tokugawa Ieyasu's campaigns to consolidate power and establish his dominance over rival daimyo and warlords. Hanzo's mastery of espionage and covert operations proved invaluable in these endeavors, as he employed a network of spies, informants, and assassins to gather intelligence and eliminate threats to the Tokugawa clan.

One of Hattori Hanzo's most famous exploits occurred during the Battle of Sekigahara in 1600, a pivotal conflict that would determine the fate of Japan. Hanzo played a crucial role in securing Tokugawa Ieyasu's victory by leading a daring night raid on the enemy camp, disrupting their supply lines and sowing confusion among their ranks.

Overall Win and Lose

Hattori Hanzo's legacy as a master of espionage and covert operations endures to this day, inspiring admiration and fascination among historians, martial artists, and enthusiasts of Japanese history and culture. While he achieved considerable success as a warrior and strategist, his ultimate victory was securing the rise to power of Tokugawa Ieyasu and the establishment of the Tokugawa shogunate, which ushered in a period of stability and prosperity for Japan.

Despite his many accomplishments, Hattori Hanzo's life was not without its share of challenges and setbacks. He faced formidable enemies and dangerous adversaries throughout his career, risking life and limb in service to his lord and clan. Yet, through his courage, skill, and unwavering loyalty, Hanzo emerged victorious, leaving behind a legacy that continues to inspire awe and admiration centuries after his death.

Death

Hattori Hanzo died in 1596 at the age of 54, having served Tokugawa Ieyasu faithfully until the end of his life. His death marked the passing of a legendary figure in Japanese history, but his legacy lived on through his descendants and the countless stories and legends that celebrated his exploits.

Interesting Facts and Figures

- Hattori Hanzo's mastery of ninjutsu, or ninja warfare, made him a feared and respected figure on the battlefield. He was renowned for his stealth, cunning, and ability to infiltrate enemy territory undetected.
- Hanzo's legendary swordsmanship earned him the nickname "Oni no Hanzo," or "Hanzo the Demon," among his enemies. He was said to wield his katana with deadly precision, striking fear into the hearts of those who dared to oppose him.
- Hattori Hanzo's exploits have been immortalized in Japanese folklore, literature, and popular culture, where he is celebrated as a symbol of loyalty, honor, and martial prowess. He has been the subject of numerous films, television series, and works of fiction, ensuring that his legend lives on for future generations to admire and emulate.
- Despite his fearsome reputation as a warrior, Hattori Hanzo was also known for his humility, integrity, and sense of duty.

He remained loyal to Tokugawa Ieyasu and the Tokugawa clan throughout his life, sacrificing his ambitions for the greater good of his lord and country.

In conclusion, Hattori Hanzo's life was defined by his unwavering loyalty to Tokugawa Ieyasu, his mastery of martial arts and ninjutsu, and his pivotal role in shaping the course of Japanese history during the tumultuous Sengoku period. He remains a revered and iconic figure in Japanese culture, admired for his courage, skill, and unwavering devotion to his lord and clan.

20

Hernan Cortés (Spain)

Hernan Cortés, a Spanish conquistador, is renowned for his conquest of the Aztec Empire in Mexico, which marked the beginning of Spanish colonization in the Americas. Cortés's expedition, known as the Spanish conquest of the Aztec Empire, led to the downfall of the powerful Aztec civilization and established Spain's dominance in the region. His conquest is one of the most significant events in world history, reshaping the course of both European and indigenous American societies.

Birth

Hernan Cortés was born in 1485 in the town of Medellin, in the Kingdom of Castile, part of modern-day Spain. He was born into a noble family of minor landowners, with modest means and aspirations. From a young age, Cortés displayed an adventurous spirit and a thirst for glory, traits that would shape his future exploits as a conquistador.

Early Life and Education

Cortés received a traditional education befitting a young nobleman of his time, studying Latin, rhetoric, and philosophy. However, he showed little interest in scholarly pursuits and instead longed for adventure and excitement. At the age of 14, Cortés left home to attend the University of Salamanca, but he soon grew restless and abandoned his studies to seek his fortune in the New World.

In 1504, at the age of 19, Cortés set sail for Hispaniola, the Spanish colony in the Caribbean, where he hoped to find wealth and glory as a conquistador. Over the next decade, he distinguished himself as a soldier and administrator, participating in expeditions and campaigns against indigenous peoples in the Caribbean and Central America.

Wars

Cortés's most famous military campaign began in 1519 when he led an expedition to explore and conquer the rich and powerful Aztec Empire in present-day Mexico. Despite facing overwhelming odds and formidable obstacles, Cortés and his small band of Spanish soldiers, along with indigenous allies, managed to defeat the Aztec forces and capture their capital city of Tenochtitlan in 1521.

The Spanish conquest of the Aztec Empire was marked by brutal warfare, political intrigue, and alliances with rival indigenous groups opposed to Aztec rule. Cortés skillfully exploited divisions among the native peoples of Mexico, playing rival factions against each other and capitalizing on their resentment towards Aztec domination.

One of Cortés's most famous military victories came at the Battle of Otumba in 1520, where his forces defeated a much larger Aztec army, despite being heavily outnumbered. The battle marked a turning point in the Spanish conquest of Mexico and demonstrated Cortés's strategic acumen and leadership on the battlefield.

Despite his military successes, Cortés faced numerous challenges and setbacks during his campaign to conquer the Aztec Empire. He struggled to maintain control over his unruly troops, who were often motivated more by greed and ambition than loyalty to their commander. Cortés also faced resistance from indigenous groups opposed to Spanish rule, as well as political opposition from rivals within the Spanish colonial administration.

Overall Win and Lose

Hernan Cortés's conquest of the Aztec Empire was a stunning military achievement that brought vast wealth and territory under Spanish control. His victory marked the beginning of Spanish dominance in the

Americas and laid the foundations for the Spanish colonial empire in the New World. However, Cortés's legacy is a complex and controversial one, marked by both triumph and tragedy.

While Cortés achieved his primary objective of conquering the Aztec Empire, his methods were ruthless and often brutal. He and his men committed numerous atrocities against the indigenous peoples of Mexico, including massacres, enslavement, and the destruction of temples and sacred sites. Cortés's actions sparked a wave of resistance and rebellion among the native populations, leading to decades of conflict and bloodshed in the region.

Despite his military successes, Cortés faced opposition and criticism from both his Spanish superiors and his indigenous allies. He was accused of insubordination, disobedience, and abuse of power, and he was eventually removed from his position as governor of New Spain in 1529.

In the years following his conquest of the Aztec Empire, Cortés's influence and power waned, as he became embroiled in legal disputes and political intrigues in Spain. He spent the remaining years of his life defending his actions in Mexico and seeking recognition and rewards for his service to the Spanish crown.

Death

Hernan Cortés died on December 2, 1547, in Seville, Spain, at the age of 62. Despite his achievements as a conquistador and explorer, Cortés's final years were marked by disappointment and disillusionment. He died a wealthy but embittered man, overshadowed by the controversy and criticism surrounding his conquest of the Aztec Empire.

Interesting Facts and Figures

- Hernan Cortés's conquest of the Aztec Empire brought vast wealth and riches to Spain, including gold, silver, and precious jewels plundered from Aztec temples and treasuries.

- Cortés's conquest of Mexico was facilitated by the assistance of indigenous allies, including the Tlaxcalans, who provided crucial support and manpower to the Spanish forces.
- Despite his military successes, Cortés's conquest of the Aztec Empire was not without its challenges and setbacks. He faced fierce resistance from the Aztec emperor Moctezuma II and his warriors, as well as from rival Spanish conquistadors and colonial administrators.
- Cortés's legacy is a complex and controversial one, with historians and scholars debating his motivations, methods, and impact on the indigenous peoples of Mexico. While some view him as a heroic explorer and conqueror, others condemn him as a ruthless imperialist who brought death and destruction to the New World.

In conclusion, Hernan Cortés's conquest of the Aztec Empire was a watershed moment in world history, reshaping the course of both European and indigenous American societies. His legacy as a conquistador and explorer is a testament to the power of ambition, determination, and ruthlessness in the pursuit of wealth and glory. However, Cortés's conquest also brought untold suffering and devastation to the native peoples of Mexico, leaving a legacy of violence and exploitation that continues to resonate to this day.

21

Horatio Nelson (England)

Horatio Nelson, 1st Viscount Nelson, is widely regarded as one of the greatest naval commanders in history. Born into a modest English family, Nelson rose through the ranks of the Royal Navy to become a legendary figure renowned for his strategic brilliance, bold leadership, and indomitable courage. His decisive victories during the Napoleonic Wars ensured British naval supremacy and secured his place in the annals of military history as a national hero.

Birth

Horatio Nelson was born on September 29, 1758, in Burnham Thorpe, Norfolk, England. He was the sixth of eleven children born to the Reverend Edmund Nelson and his wife, Catherine Suckling. From a young age, Nelson showed a keen interest in the sea and naval affairs, influenced by his uncle, Captain Maurice Suckling, who was a senior officer in the Royal Navy.

Early Life and Education

Nelson's early years were shaped by his family's connections to the sea and the naval tradition. At the age of 12, he joined the Royal Navy as a volunteer aboard the HMS Raisonnable, under the command of his uncle, Captain Suckling. Nelson's early experiences at sea laid the foundation for his future career as a naval officer and instilled in him a deep sense of duty, patriotism, and ambition.

Despite his humble origins, Nelson's talent and determination quickly caught the attention of his superiors, and he rose rapidly through the ranks of the Royal Navy. He received a comprehensive education in seamanship, navigation, and naval tactics, honing his skills through practical experience and study.

Wars

Nelson's career as a naval officer coincided with a period of intense conflict and warfare known as the Napoleonic Wars (1803-1815), which pitted Britain against the forces of Napoleon Bonaparte's French Empire. Nelson played a pivotal role in securing British naval supremacy and thwarting Napoleon's ambitions for conquest and domination.

One of Nelson's most famous victories came at the Battle of Trafalgar on October 21, 1805, off the coast of Spain. Leading a British fleet against a combined Franco-Spanish force, Nelson devised a bold and innovative strategy that would become his trademark "Nelson's patent bridge." By dividing his fleet into two columns and attacking the enemy line perpendicularly, Nelson ensured a decisive victory that shattered Napoleon's maritime ambitions and cemented British dominance of the seas.

Throughout his career, Nelson distinguished himself in numerous naval engagements and campaigns, earning a reputation for daring and audacity. His victories at the Battle of the Nile in 1798 and the Battle of Copenhagen in 1801 further solidified his status as a national hero and a symbol of British naval power.

Overall Win and Lose

Horatio Nelson's naval career was marked by numerous victories and triumphs, but it was also punctuated by setbacks and challenges. While he achieved unparalleled success on the battlefield, Nelson's personal life was fraught with turmoil and tragedy.

Despite his military accomplishments, Nelson's health deteriorated rapidly in the final years of his life, exacerbated by injuries sustained in battle and the stresses of command. He suffered from chronic seasickness, malaria, and respiratory problems, which took a toll on his physical and mental well-being.

Nelson's personal life was also marked by scandal and controversy. He engaged in a highly publicized affair with Emma Hamilton, the wife of his close friend, Sir William Hamilton, which scandalized polite society and strained his relationships with his colleagues and superiors.

In October 1805, just weeks after his historic victory at Trafalgar, Horatio Nelson was mortally wounded while leading the British fleet into battle against a combined French and Spanish force off the coast of Spain. He died on October 21, 1805, aboard his flagship, HMS Victory, at the age of 47. His death marked the end of an era in British naval history and cast a shadow over the nation's victory at Trafalgar.

Death

Horatio Nelson died on October 21, 1805, at the Battle of Trafalgar, having achieved immortality as one of Britain's greatest naval heroes. His death was mourned by the nation, and he was given a state funeral with full military honors. Nelson's body was interred in St. Paul's Cathedral in London, where he remains to this day, a symbol of British naval prowess and national pride.

Interesting Facts and Figures

- Nelson's victory at the Battle of Trafalgar is considered one of the greatest naval triumphs in history. Despite being outnumbered and outgunned, Nelson's innovative tactics and bold leadership ensured a decisive victory that changed the course of the Napoleonic Wars.
- Nelson's famous signal to his fleet before the Battle of Trafalgar, "England expects that every man will do his duty," has become a legendary rallying cry for British patriotism and naval tradition.
- Nelson's statue atop Nelson's Column in London's Trafalgar Square is one of the city's most iconic landmarks, commemorating his victory at the Battle of Trafalgar and his contribution to British naval history.

- Nelson's legacy as a naval commander and national hero is celebrated in countless memorials, monuments, and commemorations throughout Britain and the Commonwealth. His name adorns streets, buildings, and ships around the world, ensuring that his memory lives on for future generations.

In conclusion, Horatio Nelson's life and career exemplify the ideals of courage, leadership, and sacrifice. His victories at sea ensured British naval supremacy and secured his place as one of the greatest naval commanders in history. Despite his untimely death, Nelson's legacy endures as a symbol of British naval prowess and national pride, inspiring admiration and reverence to this day.

22

Hua Mulan (China)

Hua Mulan, often revered as the epitome of filial piety, courage, and devotion to duty, is a legendary figure in Chinese history and folklore. Her story has been celebrated for centuries through poetry, literature, theater, and film, inspiring generations with its themes of patriotism, gender equality, and the strength of the human spirit. While the exact details of her life remain shrouded in myth and legend, the tale of Hua Mulan continues to resonate with audiences around the world, transcending time and culture.

Birth

Hua Mulan is believed to have been born in China during the Northern Wei dynasty, which ruled from 386 to 534 AD, although the exact dates of her birth and death are unknown. According to legend, she was born into a family of modest means in the northern region of the country, near the border with Mongolia. Little is known about her early life, but she is said to have been raised with a strong sense of duty, honor, and patriotism.

Early Life and Education

As a young girl, Hua Mulan displayed a keen intelligence, a fierce independent spirit, and a natural talent for martial arts. Despite living in a patriarchal society that placed strict limitations on women's roles and freedoms, Mulan defied convention and embraced her unconventional interests and abilities.

Legend has it that Mulan's father, a retired soldier, was called to serve in the army when the Emperor issued a decree conscripting one man from each family to join the military. However, knowing that her father was elderly and infirm, and had no brothers to take his place, Mulan made the courageous decision to disguise herself as a man and take her father's place in the army.

Wars

Hua Mulan's most famous exploits occurred during her service in the army, where she distinguished herself as a skilled warrior and a fearless leader. Disguised as a man, Mulan joined the army and embarked on a journey that would test her courage, determination, and loyalty to her country.

Mulan's military career is best known for her participation in the defense of China against the invading forces of the nomadic tribes of the Northern Wei dynasty. She fought alongside her fellow soldiers in numerous battles and campaigns, displaying exceptional bravery and martial prowess on the battlefield.

One of the most famous episodes in Mulan's story is her heroic defense of her unit during a critical battle. Despite being outnumbered and outmatched by the enemy forces, Mulan rallied her comrades and led a daring charge that turned the tide of battle in favor of the Chinese army. Her leadership and valor earned her the respect and admiration of her fellow soldiers and commanders.

Throughout her military service, Mulan kept her true identity hidden, maintaining the facade of a dutiful and courageous soldier. Despite the hardships and dangers she faced, Mulan remained steadfast in her commitment to her country and her family, embodying the virtues of loyalty, sacrifice, and honor.

Overall Win and Lose

The legend of Hua Mulan is a tale of triumph against adversity, as she overcame gender barriers, societal expectations, and the challenges of war to serve her country with distinction. While Mulan's story is one of courage, sacrifice, and heroism, it is also a reflection of the struggles and injustices faced by women in traditional Chinese society.

Despite her remarkable achievements, Mulan's true identity was eventually revealed, and she was hailed as a national hero and a symbol of feminine strength and resilience. Her story has been passed down through generations, inspiring countless adaptations, interpretations, and retellings in literature, theater, and film.

Death

The exact details of Hua Mulan's death are shrouded in mystery and legend, with various versions of her story offering different accounts of her fate. Some legends suggest that Mulan retired from the military and lived out her days in peace, while others claim that she perished in battle, fighting bravely to defend her homeland.

Regardless of the circumstances of her death, Hua Mulan's legacy lives on through the countless retellings of her story and the enduring impact of her example. She remains a beloved and iconic figure in Chinese culture, celebrated for her courage, her loyalty, and her unwavering devotion to duty.

Interesting Facts and Figures

- Hua Mulan's story has been immortalized in the famous Chinese poem "Ballad of Mulan," which dates back to the 6th century AD. The poem recounts Mulan's exploits in battle and her ultimate sacrifice for her country, capturing the essence of her courage and devotion.
- Mulan's story has inspired numerous adaptations and retellings in various forms of media, including novels, plays, operas, films, and television series. Her tale has been reimagined and reinvented countless times, reflecting its enduring relevance and appeal.
- The Disney animated film "Mulan," released in 1998, brought Mulan's story to a global audience and introduced her to a new generation of fans. The film was praised for its portrayal of Mulan

as a strong, independent heroine and its celebration of Chinese culture and tradition.
- Hua Mulan's legacy extends beyond China, with her story serving as a symbol of courage, resilience, and female empowerment around the world. She remains an enduring icon of heroism and inspiration, inspiring generations with her timeless example.

In conclusion, Hua Mulan's story is a timeless testament to the power of courage, sacrifice, and devotion to duty. Her legend continues to captivate audiences around the world, serving as a source of inspiration and empowerment for people of all ages and backgrounds. Whether in poetry, literature, or film, the tale of Mulan endures as a timeless reminder of the strength and resilience of the human spirit.

23

Isabella I of Castile (Spain)

Isabella I of Castile, also known as Isabella the Catholic, was one of the most influential monarchs of the late Middle Ages. As Queen of Castile from 1474 until she died in 1504, Isabella played a pivotal role in the unification of Spain, the expansion of Spanish influence overseas, and the establishment of the Spanish Inquisition. Her reign marked a significant period of political, cultural, and religious transformation in Spain and set the stage for the rise of the Spanish Empire as a global superpower.

Birth

Isabella was born on April 22, 1451, in the town of Madrigal de las Altas Torres, in the Kingdom of Castile, which is located in present-day Spain. She was the daughter of King John II of Castile and his second wife, Isabella of Portugal. From a young age, Isabella displayed intelligence, determination, and a strong sense of religious devotion, qualities that would shape her reign as queen.

Early Life and Education

Isabella's upbringing was marked by political intrigue and instability, as the Kingdom of Castile was embroiled in internal conflicts and disputes over succession. Despite these challenges, Isabella received a comprehensive education befitting a future monarch, studying languages, history, theology, and the arts. She also received training in statecraft and diplomacy, preparing her for her future role as queen.

At the age of 17, Isabella's life took a decisive turn when she was betrothed to Ferdinand of Aragon, the heir to the neighboring Kingdom of Aragon. The marriage alliance between Isabella and Ferdinand would eventually unite the kingdoms of Castile and Aragon, laying the foundation for the unification of Spain.

Wars

Isabella's reign as queen was marked by a series of military campaigns and conflicts aimed at consolidating her power, expanding her territories, and spreading Christianity. One of the most significant military endeavors of her reign was the Reconquista or the Christian reconquest of the Iberian Peninsula from Muslim rule.

Isabella and Ferdinand waged a relentless campaign against the Muslim kingdoms of Granada, the last remaining stronghold of Islamic rule in Spain. After years of siege and warfare, the city of Granada fell to the Christian forces in 1492, marking the end of Muslim rule in Spain and the completion of the Reconquista. Isabella's victory at Granada solidified her reputation as a devout defender of the Catholic faith and earned her the title "Isabella the Catholic."

Another major military achievement of Isabella's reign was the colonization of the Americas. In 1492, Isabella and Ferdinand sponsored the expedition of Christopher Columbus, which resulted in the discovery of the New World. Isabella's support for Columbus's voyage laid the groundwork for Spanish colonization in the Americas and established Spain as a major colonial power.

Overall Win and Lose

Isabella's reign as queen was marked by both triumphs and challenges. While she achieved significant victories in the Reconquista and the colonization of the Americas, her reign was also marred by controversy and conflict, particularly in her efforts to enforce religious unity and combat heresy.

One of the most controversial aspects of Isabella's reign was her establishment of the Spanish Inquisition in 1478, a tribunal charged with rooting out heresy and enforcing religious orthodoxy. While Isabella viewed the Inquisition as a necessary measure to protect the Catholic faith and maintain social order, it led to widespread persecution, discrimination, and violence against religious minorities, particularly Jews and Muslims.

Despite these controversies, Isabella's reign saw the consolidation of Spanish power, the expansion of Spanish territories overseas, and the promotion of Catholicism as the dominant religion in Spain and its colonies. Her reign laid the foundation for the rise of the Spanish Empire as a global superpower and established Spain as a leading force in European politics and culture.

Death

Isabella died on November 26, 1504, at the age of 53, at the royal residence of the Alcázar of Medina del Campo, in Castile. Her death marked the end of an era in Spanish history and the passing of one of the most influential monarchs of the late Middle Ages. Isabella was succeeded by her daughter Joanna and her son-in-law Philip the Handsome, who would continue her legacy and further expand Spanish power and influence.

Interesting Facts and Figures

- Isabella's marriage to Ferdinand of Aragon united the kingdoms of Castile and Aragon and laid the groundwork for the unification of Spain. The union of Castile and Aragon created a powerful alliance that would dominate the politics of the Iberian Peninsula and shape the course of European history.
- Isabella's sponsorship of Christopher Columbus's voyage to the New World led to the discovery of the Americas and laid the foundation for Spanish colonization in the Western Hemisphere. Columbus's voyages opened up new trade routes, expanded European knowledge of the world, and established Spain as a major colonial power.
- Isabella's establishment of the Spanish Inquisition had far-reaching consequences for religious minorities in Spain and its

colonies. The Inquisition led to the expulsion of Jews and Muslims from Spain and the persecution of suspected heretics, contributing to a climate of fear and intolerance in Spanish society.
- Isabella's reign saw the flourishing of Spanish culture and the arts, with the patronage of artists, writers, and scholars contributing to a golden age of Spanish literature, music, and architecture. Isabella's court was a center of learning and culture, attracting intellectuals and artists from across Europe and fostering a vibrant cultural scene.

In conclusion, Isabella I of Castile was a formidable monarch whose reign left an indelible mark on Spanish history and the course of European civilization. Her achievements in politics, religion, and exploration transformed Spain into a global power and established her as one of the most influential rulers of the late Middle Ages. Despite controversies surrounding her reign, Isabella's legacy endures as a symbol of strength, determination, and devotion to duty.

24

Jan Zizka (Bohemia)

Jan Zizka, often hailed as one of the greatest military leaders of the Middle Ages, was a Bohemian general and strategist who played a pivotal role in the Hussite Wars, a series of religious conflicts that shook Central Europe in the 15th century. Zizka's innovative tactics, strategic brilliance, and unwavering commitment to the cause of the Hussites made him a legendary figure in Czech history and a symbol of resistance against foreign intervention and religious persecution.

Birth

Jan Zizka was born around the year 1360 in the village of Trocnov, located in the Kingdom of Bohemia, which is now part of the Czech Republic. Little is known about his early life, but he is believed to have come from a noble family of modest means. From a young age, Zizka showed a talent for military strategy and leadership, which would later earn him fame and renown on the battlefield.

Early Life and Education

Not much is documented about Zizka's early education, but he likely received training in martial arts and military tactics, possibly from his father or other local nobles. He may have also served as a soldier in the service of various Bohemian lords, gaining valuable experience and honing his skills as a warrior.

Wars

Jan Zizka's military career was defined by his leadership during the Hussite Wars, a series of religious conflicts that erupted in Bohemia in the early 15th century. The wars were sparked by religious and social tensions between the Catholic Church and the followers of Jan Hus, a Czech reformer who advocated for greater religious freedom and church reform.

After the death of Jan Hus in 1415, his followers, known as Hussites, rose in rebellion against the Catholic Church and the ruling elite, sparking a series of armed conflicts that would last for decades. Zizka emerged as a key leader of the Hussite movement, rallying his followers and leading them to victory against overwhelming odds.

Zizka's military genius and innovative tactics played a crucial role in the Hussite Wars, earning him a reputation as a brilliant strategist and a fearless commander. He pioneered the use of mobile, heavily armed wagons, known as "war wagons," which protected his troops while allowing them to maneuver quickly on the battlefield.

One of Zizka's most famous victories came at the Battle of Vitkov Hill in 1420, where his Hussite forces defeated a much larger Catholic army. The battle marked a turning point in the Hussite Wars and solidified Zizka's reputation as a military genius.

Overall Win and Lose

Jan Zizka's leadership and tactical brilliance were instrumental in securing a series of victories for the Hussites against their Catholic opponents. His innovative use of war wagons, combined with his strategic acumen and fearless determination, enabled the Hussites to defy the odds and hold their own against much larger and better-equipped armies.

Despite his military successes, Zizka faced numerous challenges and setbacks during the Hussite Wars. The conflict was marked by fierce fighting, brutal atrocities, and shifting alliances, as various factions vied for control of Bohemia and sought to impose their religious and political agendas on the region.

One of the greatest challenges Zizka faced was the internal divisions within the Hussite movement itself. The Hussites were divided into several factions, each with its leaders and priorities, and maintaining unity and cohesion among them proved to be a constant struggle for Zizka.

Despite these challenges, Zizka's leadership and determination ultimately proved decisive in securing victory for the Hussites. His legacy as a military leader and a national hero endures to this day, and he is remembered as one of the greatest defenders of Czech independence and religious freedom.

Death

Jan Zizka died on October 11, 1424, in the town of Přibyslav, Bohemia, at the age of 64. His death was a great loss to the Hussite cause, but his legacy lived on in the hearts and minds of his followers. Zizka was buried in the town of Tabor, where a monument was erected in his honor, commemorating his courage, leadership, and sacrifice.

Interesting Facts and Figures

- Jan Zizka's use of war wagons revolutionized medieval warfare and paved the way for the development of modern military tactics. His innovative approach to warfare allowed the Hussites to overcome their opponents' superior numbers and firepower and achieve victory against overwhelming odds.
- Zizka's leadership and military successes made him a legendary figure in Czech history and a symbol of national pride and resistance against foreign intervention and oppression. His memory is celebrated in Czech folklore, literature, and art, and his legacy continues to inspire generations of Czechs to this day.
- Zizka's military career was marked by numerous battles and campaigns, including the famous Siege of Prague in 1420, where his forces successfully defended the city against a Catholic siege. His strategic brilliance and tactical prowess were instrumental in securing victory for the Hussites and preserving their independence and religious freedom.

- Zizka's death was a great loss to the Hussite cause, but his legacy lived on in the hearts and minds of his followers. He was revered as a national hero and a symbol of Czech resistance against foreign domination and religious persecution, and his memory continues to be honored and celebrated in the Czech Republic.

In conclusion, Jan Zizka was a remarkable leader and military strategist whose contributions to the Hussite Wars had a profound and lasting impact on Czech history and culture. His innovative tactics, strategic brilliance, and unwavering commitment to the cause of religious freedom and independence made him a legendary figure in Czech history and a symbol of national pride and resilience. Zizka's legacy as a national hero and a defender of liberty continues to inspire generations of Czechs to this day, and his memory remains an enduring symbol of courage, leadership, and sacrifice.

25

Joan of Arc (France)

Joan of Arc, also known as the Maid of Orleans, is one of history's most iconic and enigmatic figures. Born into a humble peasant family in the early 15th century, Joan rose from obscurity to become a national heroine of France and a symbol of resistance against foreign invaders during the Hundred Years' War. Her remarkable story is a testament to her unwavering faith, courage, and conviction, as well as the enduring power of her legacy.

Birth

Joan of Arc was born on January 6, 1412, in the village of Domrémy, in the duchy of Bar, which was then part of the Kingdom of France. She was the daughter of Jacques d'Arc and Isabelle Romée, simple peasant farmers who lived in the rural countryside of northeastern France. From a young age, Joan displayed piety, humility, and a strong sense of religious devotion, traits that would shape her destiny.

Early Life and Education

Little is known about Joan's early education, but she was taught to read and write by her mother and received religious instruction from the local parish priest. From an early age, Joan claimed to experience visions and hear voices, which she believed to be messages from God and the saints, urging her to take up a divine mission to save France from its enemies.

Joan's devout faith and sense of destiny set her apart from her peers and fueled her determination to fulfill her divine mission, despite the challenges and obstacles she would face.

Wars

Joan of Arc's most famous exploits occurred during the Hundred Years' War, a protracted conflict between England and France that lasted from 1337 to 1453. At the time of Joan's birth, France was embroiled in a bitter struggle with England for control of the French throne, which had been contested for decades.

In 1429, at the age of just 17, Joan of Arc emerged as a key figure in the war when she presented herself to Charles VII, the Dauphin of France, and claimed to have been sent by God to help him reclaim his rightful place as king of France. Inspired by her divine mission, Charles granted Joan command of a French army and tasked her with relieving the besieged city of Orléans, which was under English control.

Joan's leadership and courage proved decisive in the Battle of Orléans, where she rallied the French troops and inspired them to victory against the English forces. The lifting of the siege of Orléans was a turning point in the Hundred Years' War and marked the beginning of a series of French victories that would eventually lead to the coronation of Charles VII as king of France.

Despite her military success, Joan's career as a military leader was short-lived. In 1430, she was captured by Burgundian forces, who were allied with the English, and sold to the English for ransom. She was subsequently put on trial by the English and their French collaborators on charges of heresy, witchcraft, and dressing in men's clothing.

Joan's trial and subsequent execution in 1431 are among the most infamous episodes in her life. Despite her courageous defense and unwavering faith, she was found guilty and sentenced to death by burning at the stake. Her martyrdom cemented her status as a symbol of French nationalism and religious devotion, and she was later canonized as a saint by the Catholic Church.

Overall Win and Lose

Joan of Arc's legacy as a military leader is mixed. While she achieved remarkable victories on the battlefield and inspired her countrymen with her courage and determination, her capture and execution by the English marked a tragic end to her military career.

In the short term, Joan's victories helped to turn the tide of the Hundred Years' War in favor of the French, paving the way for the eventual expulsion of the English from France. Her leadership and military prowess earned her a place in history as one of France's greatest heroes and a symbol of national unity and defiance against foreign oppression.

However, Joan's capture and execution dealt a significant blow to the French cause and left her countrymen without their inspirational leader. Her death was a great loss to France and a tragedy for all who had admired and supported her.

Despite her ultimate defeat on the battlefield and her untimely death, Joan of Arc's legacy endures as a symbol of courage, faith, and patriotism. She remains one of the most revered figures in French history and a source of inspiration for people around the world who admire her indomitable spirit and unwavering commitment to her beliefs.

Death

Joan of Arc was executed by burning at the stake on May 30, 1431, in the marketplace of Rouen, France, at the age of 19. Her death was a brutal and unjust end to a remarkable life, but it only served to strengthen her legacy as a martyr and a saint.

Interesting Facts and Figures

- Joan of Arc's military victories at the Battle of Orléans and other engagements helped to turn the tide of the Hundred Years' War in favor of the French and paved the way for the eventual expulsion of the English from France.
- Joan's trial and execution by the English and their French collaborators sparked outrage and condemnation throughout Europe

and fueled the flames of French nationalism and anti-English sentiment.
- Joan of Arc's canonization as a saint by the Catholic Church in 1920 cemented her status as one of the most revered figures in French history and a symbol of courage, faith, and patriotism.
- Joan's legacy continues to inspire artists, writers, and filmmakers to this day, with numerous books, plays, operas, and films depicting her life and exploits.

In conclusion, Joan of Arc's life and legacy are a testament to the power of faith, courage, and conviction. Despite her humble origins and tragic fate, she rose to become one of history's most iconic figures and a symbol of resistance against oppression and injustice. Her courage, determination, and unwavering faith continue to inspire people around the world to this day, making her a true heroine for the ages.

26

Julius Caesar (Rome)

Julius Caesar, one of history's most influential and controversial figures, was a Roman statesman, military general, and dictator who played a pivotal role in the transformation of the Roman Republic into the Roman Empire. Born into a noble family in ancient Rome, Caesar rose to prominence through his military conquests, political maneuvering, and unmatched ambition. His life and legacy have left an indelible mark on Western civilization, shaping the course of history for centuries to come.

Birth

Julius Caesar was born on July 12 or 13, 100 BCE, into a patrician family that claimed descent from the goddess Venus. His birthplace was Rome, the capital of the Roman Republic, which was then a powerful and expanding empire. Caesar's father, Gaius Caesar, was a senator and governor, while his mother, Aurelia Cotta, came from a distinguished family of consuls.

From a young age, Caesar exhibited intelligence, charisma, and ambition, traits that would serve him well in his later political and military career.

Early Life and Education

As a young man, Caesar received a thorough education in the arts, rhetoric, and philosophy, studying under some of the finest teachers in Rome. He also developed a keen interest in literature, history, and military strategy, immersing himself in the works of Greek and Roman scholars and philosophers.

In addition to his formal education, Caesar received practical training in public speaking, diplomacy, and statecraft through his involvement in Roman politics. He quickly rose through the ranks of Roman society, forging alliances with powerful politicians and aristocrats and gaining a reputation as a shrewd and ambitious young man.

Wars

Julius Caesar's military career was one of the most illustrious in ancient history, marked by a series of conquests, campaigns, and battles that expanded the boundaries of the Roman Republic and solidified his reputation as a formidable military leader.

One of Caesar's earliest military exploits was his service in Asia Minor during the Mithridatic Wars, where he distinguished himself as a brave and resourceful commander. He later served as quaestor in Spain, where he demonstrated his tactical acumen and leadership skills in battle.

Caesar's most famous military campaign was his conquest of Gaul (modern-day France), which he undertook as proconsul of the Roman province of Gaul from 58 to 50 BCE. Over eight years, Caesar waged a relentless campaign of conquest, subjugating the various tribes and chieftains of Gaul and bringing the entire region under Roman control.

His conquest of Gaul was one of the most impressive military achievements of the ancient world, demonstrating Caesar's mastery of strategy, logistics, and diplomacy. The campaign also provided him with a vast reservoir of wealth, resources, and loyal soldiers, which he would later use to consolidate his power in Rome.

Overall Win and Lose

Julius Caesar's military conquests and political machinations made him one of the most powerful and influential figures in ancient Rome. However, his rise to power was not without its challenges and controversies, and his reign as dictator was marked by political unrest, civil strife, and ultimately, his assassination.

Caesar's victories on the battlefield brought him immense wealth, prestige, and power, but they also earned him many enemies among the Roman aristocracy, who viewed him as a threat to their interests and privileges. His decision to cross the Rubicon River with his army in 49 BCE and march on Rome, thereby igniting a civil war against his political rivals, marked a decisive turning point in Roman history.

In the ensuing civil war, Caesar emerged victorious, defeating his rivals and establishing himself as the undisputed ruler of Rome. He was appointed dictator for life in 44 BCE, effectively ending the era of the Roman Republic and ushering in a new age of imperial rule.

However, Caesar's autocratic rule and his attempts to centralize power in his own hands alienated many of his former supporters and allies, leading to growing resentment and opposition. His assassination on the Ides of March (March 15), 44 BCE, by a group of conspirators led by Brutus and Cassius, marked the end of his reign and plunged Rome into another period of political turmoil and uncertainty.

Death

Julius Caesar was assassinated on March 15, 44 BCE, in the Theatre of Pompey in Rome, at the age of 56. His death was a dramatic and tumultuous event that sent shockwaves throughout the Roman world and set the stage for the collapse of the Roman Republic.

Interesting Facts and Figures

- Julius Caesar was a prolific writer and historian, producing numerous works on a wide range of subjects, including military strategy, political philosophy, and Roman history. His Commentaries on the Gallic War and the Civil War are considered classics of ancient literature and provide invaluable insights into the politics and warfare of the time.
- Caesar's assassination on the Ides of March (March 15) has become one of the most famous events in Roman history, immortalized in countless works of literature, art, and drama.

The phrase "Beware the Ides of March" has entered the popular lexicon as a warning of impending danger or betrayal.
- Caesar's legacy as a military leader, statesman, and dictator has had a profound and lasting impact on Western civilization. His reforms and policies laid the groundwork for the transition from the Roman Republic to the Roman Empire, and his name has become synonymous with power, ambition, and political intrigue.

In conclusion, Julius Caesar's life and legacy are a testament to the complexities of power, ambition, and political leadership. He was a man of extraordinary talents and ambition, whose military conquests and political machinations reshaped the course of Roman history and laid the foundation for the rise of the Roman Empire. Despite his untimely death, Caesar's legacy endures as one of the most influential figures in Western civilization, his name forever associated with power, ambition, and the inexorable march of history.

27

Khalid ibn al-Walid (Arabia)

Khalid ibn al-Walid, often referred to as the "Sword of Allah," was one of the most renowned military commanders in Islamic history. Born into the Quraysh tribe of Mecca in Arabia, Khalid emerged as a brilliant strategist and fearless warrior during the early years of Islam. His military campaigns played a crucial role in the expansion of the Islamic empire and the spread of Islam across the Arabian Peninsula and beyond. Khalid's leadership and tactical genius earned him a lasting legacy as one of the greatest generals of all time.

Birth

Khalid ibn al-Walid was born in 592 CE in the city of Mecca, in what is now present-day Saudi Arabia. He belonged to the powerful Quraysh tribe, which held significant influence in Meccan society. Little is known about Khalid's early life, but he grew up in a society marked by tribal rivalries, trade, and religious diversity.

Early Life and Education

As a member of the Quraysh tribe, Khalid received a traditional Arab upbringing, steeped in the values of courage, honor, and loyalty. He was trained in the arts of warfare from a young age, learning to ride horses, wield weapons, and engage in hand-to-hand combat. Khalid also received an education in poetry, philosophy, and Islamic theology, which would later shape his worldview and inform his decisions as a military leader.

Despite his noble birth and martial prowess, Khalid initially remained aloof from the religious and political upheavals that swept through Arabia in the early 7th century. It was not until the rise of Islam and the emergence of the Prophet Muhammad as a spiritual and political leader that Khalid's life would take a dramatic turn.

Wars

Khalid ibn al-Walid's military career began in earnest with his conversion to Islam and his subsequent service to the Prophet Muhammad and the nascent Muslim community. His talents as a military commander quickly became evident, and he rose rapidly through the ranks of the Muslim army, earning a reputation for bravery, skill, and unwavering loyalty to the cause of Islam.

One of Khalid's most famous military campaigns was the Battle of Uhud in 625 CE, where he distinguished himself as a fearless warrior and strategic thinker. Despite facing overwhelming odds, Khalid's leadership and tactical brilliance helped to secure a victory for the Muslims against the Quraysh tribe of Mecca.

Khalid's greatest achievements, however, came during the Ridda Wars, a series of conflicts that erupted following the death of the Prophet Muhammad in 632 CE. As the newly appointed commander of the Muslim army, Khalid led a series of successful campaigns against rebel tribes and apostates who had renounced Islam and refused to pay the Islamic zakat (tax).

Under Khalid's leadership, the Muslim army achieved a string of decisive victories, defeating numerous rebel factions and consolidating the authority of the Islamic state. Khalid's military genius and unwavering commitment to Islam played a crucial role in preserving the unity and integrity of the Muslim community during a time of uncertainty and upheaval.

Overall Win and Lose

Khalid ibn al-Walid's military campaigns were marked by a series of resounding victories that helped to secure the early expansion of the

Islamic empire and establish Islam as a dominant political and religious force in the Arabian Peninsula and beyond.

His leadership and tactical brilliance played a crucial role in the success of the Muslim army against overwhelming odds, earning him a reputation as one of the greatest military commanders in history. Khalid's victories paved the way for the rapid expansion of the Islamic empire and the spread of Islam across vast territories.

However, Khalid's military career was not without its controversies and setbacks. Despite his remarkable achievements on the battlefield, he faced criticism for his ruthless tactics and harsh treatment of defeated enemies. Some historians have accused Khalid of committing atrocities against non-combatants and violating the principles of Islamic warfare.

Nevertheless, Khalid's contributions to the early Islamic empire were undeniable, and his legacy as a military leader and defender of Islam endures to this day. His strategic brilliance, courage, and unwavering commitment to the cause of Islam continue to inspire Muslims around the world.

Death

Khalid ibn al-Walid died in 642 CE at the age of 50, in the town of Homs, in present-day Syria. His death marked the end of a legendary military career that had reshaped the political and religious landscape of the Arabian Peninsula and laid the foundation for the spread of Islam across the world.

Interesting Facts and Figures

- Khalid ibn al-Walid is said to have never lost a battle in his entire military career, earning him the nickname "the Sword of Allah" among Muslims.
- Khalid's military campaigns played a crucial role in the early expansion of the Islamic empire, helping to establish Islam as a dominant political and religious force in the Arabian Peninsula and beyond.

- Khalid is revered as a hero and a role model by Muslims around the world, who celebrate his achievements and honor his memory as one of the greatest military commanders in history.
- Despite his military prowess, Khalid ibn al-Walid is also remembered for his piety, humility, and devotion to Islam. He was known for his strict adherence to Islamic principles and his unwavering commitment to the cause of Islam.

In conclusion, Khalid ibn al-Walid's life and legacy are a testament to the power of faith, courage, and determination. His military achievements and unwavering commitment to the cause of Islam helped to shape the course of history and establish Islam as a major world religion. Khalid's legacy as one of the greatest military commanders in history continues to inspire Muslims around the world, who look to him as a shining example of bravery, leadership, and devotion to the faith.

28

Leonidas I (Sparta)

Leonidas I, the legendary Spartan king, is remembered as one of the most iconic figures in ancient Greek history. Renowned for his valor, leadership, and unwavering commitment to duty, Leonidas achieved immortality through his heroic stand against the Persian invasion at the Battle of Thermopylae in 480 BCE. His name has become synonymous with courage and sacrifice, inspiring countless generations with his indomitable spirit.

Birth

Leonidas I was born around 540 BCE in Sparta, a city-state renowned for its militaristic society and legendary warriors. He belonged to the Agiad dynasty, one of the two royal families of Sparta, and was the son of King Anaxandridas II and Queen Archidamia. From a young age, Leonidas was groomed for leadership and warfare, undergoing rigorous training in the Spartan agoge, the state-sponsored education system designed to produce elite soldiers.

Early Life and Education

Leonidas grew up in the harsh and disciplined environment of Sparta, where physical fitness, martial prowess, and military excellence were highly prized. Under the guidance of Spartan instructors known as paidonomos, he learned the arts of combat, strategy, and leadership, honing his skills in preparation for his future role as king.

As a member of the royal family, Leonidas received a comprehensive education that encompassed military tactics, Spartan law, and the ideals of Spartan society. He was also instilled with the values of honor, duty, and self-sacrifice, which would shape his character and guide his actions throughout his life.

Wars

Leonidas I is best known for his leadership during the Persian Wars, a series of conflicts between the Greek city-states and the Persian Empire in the early 5th century BCE. The most famous engagement of the Persian Wars was the Battle of Thermopylae, where Leonidas and a small force of Spartan warriors made their stand against the vast army of the Persian king, Xerxes I.

In 480 BCE, Xerxes launched a massive invasion of Greece, seeking to subjugate the Greek city-states and extend his empire's reach into Europe. As the Persian army advanced southward, Leonidas and a contingent of Spartan soldiers were dispatched to defend the narrow pass of Thermopylae, which provided a natural chokepoint that could be used to halt the Persian advance.

Despite being vastly outnumbered, Leonidas and his men held their ground against the Persian onslaught, fighting with unmatched ferocity and determination. For three days, they repelled wave after wave of Persian attacks, inflicting heavy casualties on the enemy and buying valuable time for the Greek forces to prepare their defenses.

Overall Win and Lose

While the Battle of Thermopylae ended in defeat for the Greeks, it was a moral victory that showcased the bravery and resilience of Leonidas and his men. By delaying the Persian advance and inflicting significant casualties on the enemy, Leonidas bought precious time for the Greek city-states to mobilize their forces and prepare for the decisive naval battle at Salamis.

Although Leonidas and his Spartan warriors ultimately perished at Thermopylae, their sacrifice inspired the Greek allies to unite against the Persian threat and ultimately repel Xerxes' invasion. The Battle of Thermopylae became a symbol of Greek defiance and resistance, and Leonidas was immortalized as a hero of Greek freedom and independence.

Death

Leonidas I died in battle at Thermopylae in 480 BCE, fighting to the last alongside his fellow Spartans. According to legend, he refused to retreat or surrender, choosing instead to stand and fight to the death in defense of his homeland and his people. His courage and selflessness in the face of overwhelming odds have made him a symbol of heroism and valor for all time.

Interesting Facts and Figures

- Leonidas I was renowned for his physical prowess and martial skills, even by Spartan standards. He was said to have been an exceptional athlete and warrior, capable of enduring the rigors of Spartan training and leading his men into battle with unmatched courage and determination.
- The Battle of Thermopylae has been immortalized in countless works of art, literature, and film, including the famous graphic novel and film "300," which depicts the heroic stand of Leonidas and his Spartan warriors against the Persian army.
- In addition to his military achievements, Leonidas was also known for his diplomatic skills and political acumen. He played a key role in forging alliances between Sparta and other Greek city-states, and his leadership helped to strengthen the bonds of unity and cooperation among the Greeks in the face of external threats.

In conclusion, Leonidas I of Sparta was a legendary figure whose courage, leadership, and sacrifice left an indelible mark on the annals of history. His heroic stand at the Battle of Thermopylae epitomizes the Spartan ethos of duty, honor, and self-sacrifice, and his legacy continues to inspire generations with its timeless message of courage and defiance in the face of tyranny. Leonidas will forever be remembered as a true hero of ancient Greece, whose name will live on in the annals of history for all time.

29

Masamune Date (Japan)

Masamune Date, also known as Date Masamune, was a prominent Japanese feudal lord and daimyo during the Sengoku period and the early Edo period. Renowned for his military prowess, political acumen, and distinctive eyepatch, Masamune was a central figure in the unification of Japan and the transition from the tumultuous Sengoku era to the stable Edo period. His leadership, ambition, and cultural patronage left a lasting impact on Japanese history and culture, earning him a place among Japan's most iconic figures.

Birth

Masamune Date was born on September 5, 1567, in Yonezawa Castle, in the province of Mutsu (present-day Miyagi Prefecture), Japan. He was the eldest son of Date Terumune, a powerful daimyo of the Date clan, who ruled over the region of Tohoku in northern Japan. From a young age, Masamune was groomed for leadership and trained in the arts of warfare, politics, and diplomacy, as befitting his status as the heir to the Date clan.

Early Life and Education

Masamune received a comprehensive education that encompassed martial arts, military strategy, literature, and the Confucian principles of governance. He studied under the tutelage of renowned scholars and martial arts masters, honing his skills in preparation for his future role as a daimyo and military leader.

As a young man, Masamune distinguished himself in battle, demonstrating courage, skill, and strategic thinking beyond his years. He quickly rose through the ranks of the Date clan, earning the respect and loyalty of his followers through his leadership on the battlefield and his vision for the future of his domain.

Wars

Masamune Date's rise to prominence coincided with one of the most turbulent periods in Japanese history—the Sengoku period, or "Age of Warring States." During this time, Japan was torn apart by civil war, as powerful daimyo vied for control of the country and sought to unify it under their rule.

Masamune proved himself to be a formidable military commander, leading his clan to victory in numerous battles and expanding their territory through conquest and diplomacy. He was known for his bold and innovative tactics, as well as his ability to inspire loyalty and devotion among his troops.

One of Masamune's most famous military campaigns was the Siege of Odawara in 1590, where he fought alongside the powerful warlord Toyotomi Hideyoshi in his campaign to unify Japan. Masamune's skillful leadership and valor in battle earned him the respect of his allies and the fear of his enemies, solidifying his reputation as one of the preeminent daimyo of his time.

Overall Win and Lose

Masamune Date's military campaigns were marked by a mixture of victories and defeats, as was common during the tumultuous Sengoku period. While he achieved significant successes in expanding his territory and consolidating his power in northern Japan, Masamune also faced setbacks and challenges along the way.

One of Masamune's most notable defeats occurred during the Battle of Sekigahara in 1600, a pivotal conflict that determined the outcome of the struggle for control of Japan. Masamune initially sided with the Western Army, led by the daimyo Ishida Mitsunari, but later switched sides to join the Eastern Army, led by Tokugawa Ieyasu. Despite his efforts, Masamune's forces were unable to turn the tide of battle, and the Eastern Army emerged victorious, paving the way for Tokugawa Ieyasu to become the undisputed ruler of Japan.

Despite his defeat at Sekigahara, Masamune remained a powerful and influential figure in Japanese politics and society. He continued to rule over his domain in northern Japan, known as the Date domain, and played a key role in the early years of the Tokugawa shogunate, serving as a trusted advisor to the Tokugawa regime.

Death

Masamune Date died on June 27, 1636, at the age of 68, in Sendai Castle, the seat of his domain in present-day Miyagi Prefecture, Japan. He was succeeded by his son, Date Tadamune, who continued his father's legacy as the ruler of the Date clan and a prominent figure in Japanese history.

Interesting Facts and Figures

- Masamune Date was known for his distinctive eyepatch, which he wore after losing his right eye to smallpox during childhood. Despite his disability, Masamune never let it hinder him in battle, and he continued to lead his troops with courage and determination.
- Masamune was also known as a patron of the arts and culture, supporting the development of literature, poetry, and the tea ceremony in his domain. He was a skilled calligrapher and poet himself, composing numerous poems that reflected his thoughts on war, leadership, and the human condition.
- Masamune's legacy as a military leader and statesman continues to be celebrated in Japan to this day. He is remembered as one of the greatest daimyo of the Sengoku period, whose courage, leadership, and vision helped to shape the course of Japanese history.

In conclusion, Masamune Date was a towering figure in Japanese history, whose leadership, ambition, and cultural patronage left an indelible mark on Japanese society. His military exploits and political achievements during the turbulent Sengoku period helped to lay the foundation for the stability and prosperity of the Tokugawa shogunate. Masamune's legacy as a warrior, statesman, and patron of the arts continues to inspire admiration and respect in Japan and around the world.

30

Miyamoto Musashi (Japan)

Miyamoto Musashi, often referred to as Japan's greatest swordsman, was a legendary samurai warrior, philosopher, and strategist who lived during the tumultuous era of the late 16th and early 17th centuries in Japan. Renowned for his unparalleled skill in swordsmanship and his unconventional approach to combat, Musashi became a mythical figure in Japanese folklore and a symbol of martial excellence. His life and teachings continue to inspire martial artists and practitioners of bushido, the samurai code of honor, to this day.

Birth

Miyamoto Musashi was born in the village of Miyamoto in the province of Mimasaka (present-day Okayama Prefecture) in Japan, in 1584. He was born into a samurai family, but his early years were marked by tragedy and upheaval. Musashi's father, Shinmen Munisai, was a skilled swordsman and martial artist, but he passed away when Musashi was still young, leaving him orphaned and without a formal education.

Early Life and Education

Despite his lack of formal schooling, Musashi received an education in the martial arts from his father and other mentors in his village. From a young age, he showed a natural talent for swordsmanship and a fierce determination to excel in the martial arts. Musashi's upbringing was marked by a rigorous regimen of training, discipline, and self-improvement, as he sought to master the way of the sword and become a true warrior.

As Musashi matured, he embarked on a journey of self-discovery and enlightenment, traveling throughout Japan and engaging in duels with other swordsmen to test his skills and refine his techniques. He studied various martial arts styles, including kenjutsu (swordsmanship), jujutsu (unarmed combat), and tactics, drawing inspiration from both traditional and unconventional sources.

Wars

Miyamoto Musashi lived during a period of intense political upheaval and social unrest in Japan, known as the Sengoku period, or "Age of Warring States." During this time, Japan was fragmented into numerous feuding states and factions, locked in a constant struggle for power and dominance.

Musashi's martial prowess and skill in combat quickly gained him a reputation as a formidable warrior, and he became embroiled in the conflicts and wars that defined the era. He fought in several battles and skirmishes, both as a soldier and as a freelance mercenary, demonstrating his courage, skill, and tactical genius on the battlefield.

One of Musashi's most famous exploits occurred during the Battle of Sekigahara in 1600, a decisive conflict that determined the future course of Japanese history. Although Musashi was not a central figure in the battle, his martial prowess and reputation as a swordsman earned him a place in the annals of Japanese military history.

Overall Win and Lose

Miyamoto Musashi's martial career was marked by numerous victories and triumphs, as well as occasional setbacks and defeats. He was undefeated in over sixty duels and skirmishes throughout his life, earning him a reputation as the greatest swordsman of his time.

Musashi's unconventional approach to combat, which emphasized adaptability, intuition, and psychological warfare, set him apart from other warriors of his era. He believed in using whatever means necessary to achieve victory, whether through superior skill, strategy, or sheer force of will.

Despite his martial prowess, Musashi was not immune to failure or adversity. He faced numerous challenges and obstacles throughout his life, including personal struggles and inner demons. However, he persevered through adversity, drawing strength from his experiences and using them to fuel his personal growth and development as a warrior and as a human being.

Death

Miyamoto Musashi died on June 13, 1645, at the age of 60, in the village of Higo, in present-day Kumamoto Prefecture, Japan. He passed away peacefully, surrounded by his disciples and followers, having achieved a state of enlightenment and inner peace in his final years.

Interesting Facts and Figures

- Miyamoto Musashi is best known for his treatise on martial strategy and philosophy, "The Book of Five Rings" (Gorin no Sho). Written in the final years of his life, the book outlines Musashi's teachings on swordsmanship, strategy, and the principles of bushido, the samurai code of honor.
- Musashi was also a skilled artist and calligrapher, and his works are considered masterpieces of Japanese ink painting and brushwork. He often incorporated his artistic talents into his martial training, viewing them as complementary disciplines that helped to cultivate his mind, body, and spirit.
- Musashi's legacy as a swordsman and philosopher continues to resonate in Japan and around the world. He is revered as a cultural icon and a symbol of martial excellence, inspiring generations of martial artists and practitioners of bushido to strive for perfection in their chosen pursuits.

In conclusion, Miyamoto Musashi was a towering figure in Japanese history and martial arts, whose life and teachings continue to inspire and captivate people to this day. His unparalleled skill in swordsmanship, his philosophical insights, and his unwavering commitment to the way of the warrior have earned him a place of honor in the annals of Japanese culture and history. Musashi's legacy as a true master of the martial arts endures as a testament to the power of discipline, dedication, and self-mastery.

31

Mustafa Kemal Atatürk (Turkey)

Mustafa Kemal Atatürk, born Mustafa Kemal, is one of the most influential figures in modern Turkish history. He was a visionary statesman, military leader, and reformer who played a pivotal role in the founding of the Republic of Turkey and the transformation of the Ottoman Empire into a secular, modern nation-state. Atatürk's leadership, progressive reforms, and enduring legacy have left an indelible mark on Turkey and continue to shape its identity to this day.

Birth

Mustafa Kemal Atatürk was born on either March 12th or 20th, 1881, in the town of Salonica (Thessaloniki) in the Ottoman Empire, which is now part of Greece. He was born into a middle-class family, the son of Ali Riza Efendi, a customs officer, and Zubeyde Hanim. Atatürk received his early education in Salonica, where he displayed exceptional intelligence and leadership qualities from a young age.

Early Life and Education

As a young man, Mustafa Kemal excelled in his studies, particularly in mathematics and literature. He attended military schools in Salonica and later enrolled in the prestigious Ottoman Military Academy in Istanbul, where he received formal military training. Despite facing financial difficulties, Mustafa Kemal distinguished himself as a brilliant student and a natural leader among his peers.

Upon graduating from the Military Academy, Mustafa Kemal embarked on a distinguished military career, rising through the ranks of the Ottoman Army and earning a reputation as a courageous and resourceful officer. He served in various military campaigns and conflicts, including the Balkan Wars and World War I, where he demonstrated his strategic acumen and battlefield prowess.

Wars

Mustafa Kemal's military career reached its zenith during World War I when he emerged as a national hero and a symbol of Turkish resistance against foreign intervention. He played a pivotal role in the Gallipoli Campaign of 1915, where Ottoman forces successfully repelled an Allied invasion of the Gallipoli Peninsula, inflicting heavy casualties on the British, Australian, and New Zealand troops.

Following the Ottoman Empire's defeat in World War I, Mustafa Kemal emerged as the leader of the Turkish nationalist movement, which sought to resist foreign occupation and preserve the territorial integrity of Anatolia. In 1919, he convened the Congress of Erzurum and the Congress of Sivas, where he laid the groundwork for the establishment of a new Turkish state based on the principles of national sovereignty and popular sovereignty.

Overall Win and Lose

Mustafa Kemal's leadership and military prowess played a decisive role in the Turkish War of Independence, which lasted from 1919 to 1923. Despite facing overwhelming odds and numerous setbacks, including occupation by Allied forces and internal divisions among Turkish nationalists, Mustafa Kemal rallied the Turkish people to resist foreign domination and fight for their independence.

Under Mustafa Kemal's leadership, Turkish forces achieved a series of decisive victories against Allied occupiers and Greek invaders, culminating in the Treaty of Lausanne in 1923, which recognized the sovereignty of the Republic of Turkey and established its modern borders. Mustafa Kemal's leadership during the War of Independence solidified his reputation as a national hero and earned him the title of Atatürk, or "Father of the Turks."

Death

Mustafa Kemal Atatürk passed away on November 10, 1938, at the age of 57, in Dolmabahçe Palace in Istanbul, Turkey. His death marked the end of an era and the passing of a visionary leader who had dedicated his life to the transformation of Turkey into a modern, secular republic.

Interesting Facts and Figures

- Atatürk's legacy as a reformer and modernizer is evident in the sweeping reforms he implemented during his tenure as Turkey's first president. These reforms, known as the Kemalist Reforms, aimed to modernize Turkish society and institutions, promote secularism and Westernization and create a more egalitarian and democratic society.
- Among Atatürk's most significant reforms were the abolition of the Ottoman sultanate and the establishment of a secular republic, the introduction of the Latin alphabet to replace the Arabic script, and the adoption of European legal codes and educational systems. He also implemented measures to promote gender equality, including granting women the right to vote and run for office.
- Atatürk's legacy extends beyond Turkey's borders, as he is revered as a symbol of modernization and progressivism in the Muslim world. His reforms and vision for a secular, democratic society continue to inspire reformers and activists in the Middle East and beyond.

In conclusion, Mustafa Kemal Atatürk was a transformative figure whose leadership, vision, and courage reshaped the course of Turkish history. His legacy as the founder of the Republic of Turkey and the architect of its modernization and secularization continues to be celebrated in Turkey and admired around the world. Atatürk's enduring influence serves as a reminder of the power of leadership and the ability of individuals to shape the destiny of nations.

32

Napoleon Bonaparte (France)

Napoleon Bonaparte, the Emperor of the French, was a towering figure of the late 18th and early 19th centuries. Born in Corsica, he rose to prominence during the tumultuous years of the French Revolution and went on to become one of history's most influential military leaders and statesmen. Napoleon's military genius, administrative reforms, and ambitious campaigns reshaped the political landscape of Europe and left an enduring legacy that continues to fascinate historians and scholars to this day.

Birth

Napoleon Bonaparte was born on August 15, 1769, in Ajaccio, Corsica, which was then part of the Republic of Genoa. He was the second of eight children born to Carlo Buonaparte and Letizia Ramolino. Despite being born into a relatively modest family of minor nobility, Napoleon's ambition, intelligence, and drive set him apart from an early age.

Early Life and Education

Napoleon received his early education at home, under the guidance of tutors and his mother, who instilled in him a love of learning and a strong sense of ambition. At the age of nine, he was sent to France to attend school in Autun and later enrolled in the prestigious military academy in Brienne-le-Château.

Napoleon's time at military school proved to be formative, as he excelled in his studies and demonstrated a keen interest in military strategy and tactics. He graduated as a second lieutenant in the artillery regiment of the French army at the age of 16 and began his military career with a commission in the Royal Artillery.

Wars

Napoleon's military career began during the French Revolution, a period of profound political and social upheaval in France. He rose through the ranks of the French army through a combination of skill, ambition, and political savvy, and quickly distinguished himself as a capable and charismatic leader.

Napoleon's military campaigns during the French Revolutionary Wars earned him widespread acclaim and recognition as a brilliant tactician and strategist. He achieved a series of stunning victories against France's enemies, including the Austrians, Prussians, and Italians, culminating in his conquest of northern Italy and the signing of the Treaty of Campo Formio in 1797.

In 1799, Napoleon staged a coup d'état and seized power in France, establishing himself as First Consul and effectively becoming the ruler of France. Over the next decade, he embarked on a series of ambitious military campaigns known as the Napoleonic Wars, which would ultimately reshape the political map of Europe.

Overall Win and Lose

Napoleon's military campaigns during the Napoleonic Wars were marked by both triumphs and setbacks. He achieved a string of stunning victories, including the Battle of Austerlitz in 1805, the Battle of Jena-Auerstedt in 1806, and the Battle of Wagram in 1809, which solidified his reputation as one of history's greatest military commanders.

However, Napoleon's relentless pursuit of territorial expansion and his refusal to compromise with his enemies eventually led to his downfall. His ill-fated invasion of Russia in 1812, followed by his defeat at the Battle of Leipzig in 1813, weakened his grip on power and paved the way for his eventual defeat at the hands of the Allied forces in 1814.

Napoleon was forced to abdicate the throne and was exiled to the island of Elba, but he escaped and briefly reclaimed power during the Hundred Days in 1815. His final defeat came at the Battle of Waterloo, where he was decisively defeated by the Duke of Wellington and Prussian forces, leading to his second abdication and exile to the remote island of Saint Helena in the South Atlantic.

Death

Napoleon Bonaparte died on May 5, 1821, at the age of 51, on the island of Saint Helena, where he had been imprisoned by the British government since his defeat at Waterloo. His death was attributed to stomach cancer, although some historians have speculated that he may have been poisoned.

Interesting Facts and Figures

- Napoleon was a prolific writer and scholar, and he is credited with numerous military treatises, memoirs, and letters that provide valuable insights into his strategies, tactics, and thoughts on leadership.
- Napoleon's military innovations, including the use of mass conscription, rapid troop movements, and centralized command and control, revolutionized warfare and influenced military doctrine for decades to come.
- Napoleon's legacy extends beyond his military conquests and political achievements. He is also remembered for his administrative reforms, including the Napoleonic Code, which codified French law and served as the basis for legal systems in many countries around the world.

In conclusion, Napoleon Bonaparte was a complex and multifaceted figure whose life and legacy continue to fascinate and intrigue people to this day. As a military leader, statesman, and reformer, he left an indelible mark on the history of France and Europe, shaping the course of events for generations to come. While his ambitions ultimately led to his downfall, Napoleon's impact on the world remains undeniable, and his name is synonymous with ambition, conquest, and the pursuit of greatness.

33

Naresuan the Great (Siam/Thailand)

Naresuan the Great, also known as King Naresuan, was one of the most revered monarchs in Thai history. He ruled the Ayutthaya Kingdom, a powerful kingdom in Southeast Asia, during the late 16th century. Naresuan is remembered for his military prowess, diplomatic skill, and contributions to the expansion and consolidation of Siamese territory. His reign marked a golden age in Thai history and cemented his legacy as a national hero and symbol of Thai independence.

Birth

Naresuan was born on April 25, 1555, in Phitsanulok, in the northern region of Siam (present-day Thailand). He was the second son of King Maha Thammaracha, the ruler of the Ayutthaya Kingdom, and Queen Wisutkasat. From a young age, Naresuan displayed intelligence, courage, and leadership qualities that would shape his future as a great warrior and monarch.

Early Life and Education

As a member of the royal family, Naresuan received a comprehensive education befitting his status. He studied the arts of warfare, diplomacy, and statecraft under the guidance of learned scholars and military advisors appointed by his father. From an early age, Naresuan demonstrated a keen interest in military strategy and tactics, and he honed his skills through rigorous training and practical experience.

Naresuan's formative years were marked by political intrigue and dynastic rivalries within the Ayutthaya court. He endured periods of exile and captivity as a result of court intrigues, but these experiences only served to strengthen his resolve and determination to assert his rightful claim to the throne.

Wars

Naresuan ascended to the throne of the Ayutthaya Kingdom in 1590, following the death of his father, King Maha Thammaracha. His reign was characterized by a series of military campaigns aimed at expanding and consolidating Siamese territory and asserting Thai sovereignty in the face of external threats.

One of Naresuan's most famous military campaigns was his campaign against the Burmese Kingdom of Toungoo, which had long been a rival of the Ayutthaya Kingdom. In 1593, Naresuan led his forces in a series of decisive battles against the Burmese army, culminating in the legendary Battle of Nong Sarai in 1593. Naresuan's victory at Nong Sarai secured Siamese independence and established him as a national hero and champion of Thai nationalism.

Overall Win and Lose

Naresuan's military campaigns were marked by a mixture of victories and setbacks, as was common in the turbulent political landscape of Southeast Asia during the 16th century. While he achieved significant successes in expanding Siamese territory and asserting Thai sovereignty, Naresuan also faced formidable challenges from rival kingdoms and internal rebellions.

One of Naresuan's most notable defeats occurred during his invasion of the Burmese Kingdom of Ava in 1600. Despite initial successes, Naresuan's forces were eventually repelled by the Burmese army, forcing him to retreat and regroup. However, Naresuan's defeat at Ava did not diminish his stature as a military leader or dampen his determination to defend Thai independence.

Death

Naresuan the Great died on April 25, 1605, at the age of 49, in Ayutthaya, the capital of the Ayutthaya Kingdom. His death was mourned by the Thai people, who revered him as a national hero and champion of Thai independence. Naresuan's legacy endured long after his death, shaping the course of Thai history and inspiring future generations of Thai leaders and patriots.

Interesting Facts and Figures

- Naresuan the Great is remembered for his legendary rivalry with Bayinnaung, the powerful king of the Taungoo Dynasty in Burma. The two monarchs clashed in a series of epic battles that defined the political landscape of Southeast Asia during the late 16th century.
- Naresuan was a patron of the arts and culture, and his reign witnessed the flourishing of Thai literature, art, and architecture. He commissioned numerous temples, palaces, and monuments throughout the Ayutthaya Kingdom, many of which still stand as testaments to his legacy.
- Naresuan's reign marked the beginning of a golden age in Thai history, characterized by political stability, economic prosperity, and cultural achievement. His contributions to the expansion and consolidation of Siamese territory laid the foundation for the modern nation of Thailand.

In conclusion, Naresuan the Great was a legendary monarch whose reign marked a golden age in Thai history. His military prowess, diplomatic skill, and contributions to the expansion and consolidation of Siamese territory earned him a place of honor in Thai folklore and history. Naresuan's legacy as a national hero and champion of Thai independence continues to inspire reverence and admiration among the Thai people to this day.

34

Oda Nobunaga (Japan)

Oda Nobunaga was a powerful daimyo (feudal lord) and one of the most significant figures in Japanese history during the Sengoku period (the Warring States period). Known for his ruthless ambition, military genius, and innovative strategies, Nobunaga played a pivotal role in unifying Japan under his rule. His efforts laid the groundwork for the establishment of the Tokugawa shogunate and the eventual reunification of Japan.

Birth

Oda Nobunaga was born on June 23, 1534, in Nagoya Castle, in the Owari Province of central Japan. He was the second son of Oda Nobuhide, a minor daimyo in the Owari region. From a young age, Nobunaga displayed a keen intellect, strong leadership qualities, and an ambitious nature that would shape his future as a formidable warrior and statesman.

Early Life and Education

Nobunaga received a traditional samurai education, which included training in martial arts, military strategy, and the Confucian principles of governance. However, his upbringing was marked by family turmoil and political intrigue, as he vied for power and influence within his clan.

Following his father's death in 1551, Nobunaga assumed leadership of the Oda clan at the age of 17. Despite facing opposition from rival factions within the clan, Nobunaga quickly asserted his authority and set about expanding his influence in the Owari region.

Wars

Nobunaga's rise to power coincided with a period of intense political upheaval and social unrest in Japan. The country was divided into numerous warring factions, each vying for control of territory and resources. Sensing an opportunity to expand his domain, Nobunaga embarked on a series of military campaigns aimed at subduing rival daimyo and consolidating his power.

One of Nobunaga's most famous military campaigns was his conquest of the capital city of Kyoto in 1568. With the support of his ally, the shogun Ashikaga Yoshiaki, Nobunaga marched his forces into Kyoto and installed Yoshiaki as a puppet ruler. This victory solidified Nobunaga's position as a dominant force in Japanese politics and marked the beginning of his quest to unify Japan under his rule.

Overall Win and Lose

Nobunaga's military campaigns were marked by both triumphs and setbacks. He achieved significant successes in expanding his territory and defeating rival daimyo, thanks to his innovative tactics and ruthless determination. Nobunaga's use of firearms and his willingness to adopt new technologies and strategies set him apart from his contemporaries and gave him a distinct advantage on the battlefield.

However, Nobunaga's quest for dominance ultimately proved to be his undoing. Despite his military prowess, he faced formidable challenges from rival daimyo, internal rebellions, and betrayal within his ranks. His ruthless tactics and authoritarian rule also alienated many of his allies and subjects, leading to widespread resentment and opposition.

Death

Nobunaga's life came to a tragic end on June 21, 1582, at the age of 47, during the Honno-ji Incident. While staying at the Honno-ji temple in Kyoto, Nobunaga was betrayed by one of his generals, Akechi Mitsuhide, who launched a surprise attack on the temple. Facing overwhelming odds, Nobunaga chose to commit seppuku (ritual suicide) rather than be captured or killed by his enemies.

Interesting Facts and Figures

- Nobunaga was known for his progressive policies and his efforts to modernize and centralize the administration of his domains. He encouraged trade and commerce, promoted the arts and culture, and implemented land reforms to improve agricultural productivity and stimulate economic growth.
- Nobunaga's patronage of the arts and his support for tea ceremony masters, painters, and artisans helped to foster a vibrant cultural renaissance in Japan. His enthusiasm for Western-style architecture and firearms also had a profound impact on Japanese society and culture.
- Despite his reputation as a ruthless warlord, Nobunaga was also a complex and enigmatic figure who inspired loyalty and admiration among his followers. He was revered as a visionary leader and a symbol of strength and resilience in the face of adversity.

In conclusion, Oda Nobunaga was a towering figure in Japanese history whose legacy continues to resonate to this day. His military prowess, innovative strategies, and progressive policies laid the foundation for the unification of Japan and the establishment of the Tokugawa shogunate. While his life ended in tragedy, Nobunaga's impact on Japanese politics, society, and culture cannot be overstated, and he remains a revered and iconic figure in Japanese folklore and history.

35

Rani Lakshmibai (India)

Rani Lakshmibai, also known as the Rani of Jhansi, was a fearless warrior queen and one of the most prominent figures of the Indian Rebellion of 1857. Born into a noble family in India, she rose to prominence for her bravery, leadership, and unwavering commitment to the cause of Indian independence. Rani Lakshmibai's valiant efforts to resist British colonial rule have earned her a revered place in Indian history and folklore as a symbol of courage and patriotism.

Birth

Rani Lakshmibai was born Manikarnika Tambe on November 19, 1828, in the town of Varanasi, in present-day Uttar Pradesh, India. She was the daughter of Moropant Tambe, a Marathi Brahmin, and Bhagirathi Sapre. From a young age, Manikarnika exhibited a strong spirit and independent nature, traits that would serve her well in the tumultuous years to come.

Early Life and Education

Manikarnika received a traditional education befitting her noble status, which included instruction in Sanskrit, martial arts, and horse riding. She also demonstrated a keen interest in literature and poetry, and her education instilled in her a deep sense of pride in her Indian heritage and a strong belief in the principles of justice and equality.

At the age of 14, Manikarnika was married to the Maharaja of Jhansi, Gangadhar Rao Newalkar. Following her marriage, she adopted the name Lakshmibai in honor of the Hindu goddess Lakshmi, and she became known as the Rani of Jhansi.

Wars

Rani Lakshmibai's life was forever changed by the outbreak of the Indian Rebellion of 1857, also known as the Sepoy Mutiny. The rebellion was sparked by several grievances against British colonial rule, including economic exploitation, cultural imperialism, and the forced introduction of Western values and institutions.

In March 1858, British forces launched an attack on the city of Jhansi, seeking to suppress the rebellion and assert their control over the region. Despite being outnumbered and outgunned, Rani Lakshmibai rallied her forces and led a fierce resistance against the British invaders. She led her troops into battle, displaying remarkable courage and determination in the face of overwhelming odds.

Overall Win and Lose

Rani Lakshmibai's leadership during the Siege of Jhansi was characterized by both triumphs and setbacks. Despite her valiant efforts to defend her kingdom, Jhansi ultimately fell to the British forces in April 1858 after a prolonged siege. However, Rani Lakshmibai's defiance inspired other Indian leaders and freedom fighters to continue the struggle against British rule, and her legacy as a symbol of resistance and independence endures to this day.

Death

Rani Lakshmibai's life came to a tragic end on June 18, 1858, during the Battle of Gwalior. Faced with overwhelming British forces, she chose to lead a daring charge against the enemy lines, rather than surrender or retreat. In the heat of battle, Rani Lakshmibai was struck by a bullet and mortally wounded. Despite her injuries, she continued to fight bravely until her last breath, inspiring her troops to continue the struggle for freedom.

Interesting Facts and Figures

- Rani Lakshmibai's bravery and leadership during the Indian Rebellion of 1857 earned her widespread admiration and respect, both in India and abroad. She became a symbol of resistance and defiance against British colonial rule, and her memory has been immortalized in Indian folklore, literature, and popular culture.
- Rani Lakshmibai is perhaps best remembered for her iconic ride into battle, during which she reportedly fought with her infant son tied to her back. This legendary act of courage has become emblematic of her indomitable spirit and unwavering commitment to the cause of Indian independence.
- In recognition of her contributions to the struggle for Indian independence, Rani Lakshmibai is commemorated with numerous memorials, statues, and monuments throughout India. Her life and legacy continue to inspire generations of Indians to strive for justice, equality, and freedom.

In conclusion, Rani Lakshmibai was a true heroine of Indian history, whose courage, determination, and sacrifice continue to inspire people around the world. Her unwavering commitment to the cause of Indian independence and her fearless defiance of British colonial rule have earned her a revered place in the annals of Indian history as a symbol of courage, patriotism, and resistance.

36

Red Cloud (Lakota Sioux)

Red Cloud, a prominent leader of the Oglala Lakota Sioux, emerged as a central figure in the resistance against the encroachment of white settlers and the United States government into Native American lands during the 19th century. Born during a time of great change and upheaval for Indigenous peoples, Red Cloud rose to prominence through his military prowess, diplomatic skills, and unwavering commitment to defending the ancestral lands of his people against colonial expansion.

Birth

Red Cloud, whose Lakota name was Mahpíya Lúta, was born in 1822 near the forks of the Platte River, in present-day Nebraska. He was born into the Oglala band of the Lakota Sioux, a nomadic Plains Indian tribe known for their warrior culture, horsemanship, and deep spiritual beliefs. From an early age, Red Cloud exhibited leadership qualities and a keen sense of his people's heritage and traditions.

Early Life and Education

As a young man, Red Cloud received traditional education and training in the skills necessary for survival on the Great Plains, including hunting, tracking, and warfare. He learned the art of diplomacy and negotiation from tribal elders and experienced warriors, who passed down the oral traditions and wisdom of their ancestors.

Red Cloud's early years were marked by conflict and upheaval, as white settlers and U.S. government officials began to encroach on

Lakota territory in search of land, resources, and gold. Witnessing the rapid transformation of the Plains and the growing threat to his people's way of life, Red Cloud became determined to defend Lakota's sovereignty and preserve their ancestral lands.

Wars

Red Cloud rose to prominence as a military leader during the conflicts between the Lakota Sioux and the United States government in the mid-19th century. In the early 1860s, tensions between the Lakota and the U.S. Army escalated into open warfare as white settlers encroached further onto Lakota lands and violated treaties negotiated with the tribes.

One of Red Cloud's most significant military achievements came during Red Cloud's War (1866-1868), a protracted conflict between the Lakota Sioux and the U.S. Army over control of the Powder River Country in present-day Wyoming and Montana. Red Cloud's forces, consisting of warriors from various Lakota bands, launched a series of raids and ambushes against U.S. military outposts, supply trains, and settlements, inflicting heavy casualties and disrupting the government's efforts to establish control over the region.

Overall Win and Lose

Red Cloud's leadership during Red Cloud's War was instrumental in forcing the U.S. government to negotiate a peace treaty known as the Treaty of Fort Laramie in 1868. The treaty guaranteed the Lakota Sioux exclusive control over the Black Hills of South Dakota and a large portion of the Powder River Country, effectively recognizing Lakota sovereignty over their ancestral lands.

However, the peace achieved through the Treaty of Fort Laramie was short-lived, as the discovery of gold in the Black Hills soon led to renewed conflict between the Lakota Sioux and the United States government. Despite his efforts to uphold the terms of the treaty and maintain peace, Red Cloud was ultimately unable to prevent the U.S. government from violating its provisions and forcibly seizing Lakota territory.

Death

Red Cloud lived to see the devastating consequences of the U.S. government's betrayal of the Treaty of Fort Laramie and the continued encroachment of white settlers onto Lakota lands. He passed away on December 10, 1909, at the age of 87, on the Pine Ridge Indian Reservation in South Dakota. Despite the hardships and challenges he faced throughout his life, Red Cloud remained a revered and respected leader among his people until his dying day.

Interesting Facts and Figures

- Red Cloud's leadership during Red Cloud's War earned him widespread admiration and respect among his people and other Plains Indian tribes. He was regarded as a skilled strategist and tactician who led his warriors with courage, determination, and integrity.
- Red Cloud was known for his efforts to preserve Lakota culture, traditions, and way of life in the face of relentless pressure from white settlers and the U.S. government. He advocated for the rights of Native American tribes and sought to protect their land, resources, and sovereignty.
- Red Cloud's legacy as a warrior, statesman, and defender of Indigenous rights continues to inspire Native American activists, leaders, and scholars to this day. His name is synonymous with courage, resilience, and the ongoing struggle for justice and equality for Indigenous peoples.

In conclusion, Red Cloud was a visionary leader and a fierce defender of Lakota sovereignty and culture during a time of profound change and upheaval for Indigenous peoples. His legacy as a warrior, diplomat, and advocate for Native American rights continues to resonate today, serving as a reminder of the ongoing struggle for justice, equality, and self-determination in the face of colonialism and oppression.

37

Richard the Lionheart (England)

Richard the Lionheart, also known as Richard I, was a renowned medieval monarch who ruled as King of England from 1189 until he died in 1199. He is remembered as a courageous military leader, a patron of the arts, and a central figure in the Christian Crusades. Richard's reign was marked by his military exploits, diplomatic prowess, and enduring legacy as a symbol of chivalry and medieval kingship.

Birth

Richard was born on September 8, 1157, in Oxford, England, the third son of King Henry II of England and Eleanor of Aquitaine. As a member of the Plantagenet dynasty, Richard was heir to a vast empire that included England, Normandy, Aquitaine, and other territories in France. From a young age, Richard displayed a natural aptitude for martial pursuits, earning him the nickname "Lionheart" for his bravery and valor on the battlefield.

Early Life and Education

Richard received a comprehensive education befitting his royal status, studying history, literature, languages, and military strategy under the guidance of learned tutors and scholars. He also honed his skills in horsemanship, archery, and swordsmanship, becoming a formidable warrior and leader.

Despite his upbringing in the royal court, Richard's early years were overshadowed by tensions and rivalries within his family. He competed with his brothers for power and influence, particularly his younger brother John, who would later become King John of England.

Wars

Richard's reign was characterized by his military campaigns in Europe and the Holy Land, where he sought to expand his territories and defend Christendom against Muslim forces during the Third Crusade. One of Richard's most famous military campaigns was his participation in the Crusades, a series of religious wars aimed at reclaiming Jerusalem and other holy sites from Muslim control.

In 1189, Richard embarked on the Third Crusade alongside King Philip II of France and Emperor Frederick Barbarossa of the Holy Roman Empire. Together, they led Christian forces against the powerful Muslim sultan Saladin, engaging in a series of battles and sieges across the Levant.

Overall Win and Lose

Richard's leadership during the Third Crusade was marked by both victories and setbacks. He won several notable battles against Saladin's forces, including the decisive Battle of Arsuf in 1191, which secured a strategic victory for the Christians. However, Richard's failure to capture Jerusalem and achieve a lasting peace with Saladin ultimately led to the collapse of the Crusade and his return to Europe in 1192.

Despite the mixed outcomes of the Third Crusade, Richard's reputation as a fearless warrior and champion of Christendom endured, earning him widespread admiration and respect among his subjects and contemporaries. His military exploits in the Holy Land cemented his legacy as one of the greatest medieval monarchs and a symbol of Christian valor and chivalry.

Death

Richard the Lionheart died on April 6, 1199, at the age of 41, from a wound sustained during a siege in the Limousin region of France. His death marked the end of an era in English history and plunged the kingdom into a period of uncertainty and turmoil.

Despite his untimely death, Richard's legacy as a warrior king and patron of the arts endured long after his passing. He was succeeded by his younger brother John, whose reign was marred by conflict and controversy, contrasting sharply with the glory and prestige of Richard's rule.

Interesting Facts and Figures

- Richard the Lionheart is best known for his role in the Robin Hood legends, which depict him as a noble and honorable ruler who fought against injustice and tyranny. While the historical accuracy of these stories is debatable, they have contributed to Richard's enduring popularity and mythic status in English folklore.
- Richard was a patron of the troubadours, poets, and musicians of his court, fostering a vibrant cultural and artistic Renaissance in England. He also commissioned the construction of numerous castles, cathedrals, and fortifications, leaving a lasting architectural legacy that still stands today.
- Despite his reputation as a heroic warrior king, Richard's reign was marked by controversy and conflict, both at home and abroad. His frequent absences from England and his heavy taxation of the kingdom to fund his military campaigns alienated many of his subjects and contributed to unrest and discontent.

In conclusion, Richard the Lionheart was a legendary medieval monarch whose reign left an indelible mark on English history and the Christian world. His military prowess, diplomatic skill, and patronage of the arts helped to shape the course of European civilization and establish him as one of the most celebrated figures of the Middle Ages. Despite the challenges and controversies of his reign, Richard's legacy as a fearless warrior and chivalrous knight endures to this day, inspiring generations of historians, artists, and storytellers.

38

Rollo of Normandy (Norway/France)

Rollo of Normandy, also known as Rollo the Walker or Rollo the Viking, was a renowned Norse chieftain and the founder of the Norman dynasty in France. Born during the Viking Age, Rollo rose from humble beginnings to become one of the most influential figures of his time. He played a pivotal role in the Viking expansion into France and laid the foundation for the Norman conquest of England, leaving a lasting legacy that would shape the course of European history.

Birth

Rollo was born around the year 846 in the kingdom of Norway, during a period of Viking raids and territorial expansion throughout Europe. Little is known about his early life, but it is believed that he came from a noble lineage and received training in the martial skills and seafaring traditions of the Norsemen.

Early Life and Education

As a young man, Rollo distinguished himself as a skilled warrior and leader among his Viking peers. He participated in numerous raids and military campaigns across Europe, gaining a reputation for his ferocity in battle and his cunning tactics. Rollo's early experiences in warfare and exploration would shape his future ambitions and set him on a path to greatness.

Wars

Rollo's military career reached its zenith with the Viking invasion of France in the early 10th century. Alongside his fellow Norsemen, Rollo led a series of devastating raids along the coast of France, pillaging villages, monasteries, and towns in search of plunder and glory. The Vikings' swift and ruthless attacks struck fear into the hearts of the Frankish people and exposed the weaknesses of their defenses.

One of Rollo's most significant military campaigns was the siege of Paris in 885-886, during which he and his Viking army laid siege to the fortified city for over a year. Despite facing determined resistance from the defenders, Rollo's forces eventually breached the walls and sacked the city, extracting a hefty ransom in exchange for their withdrawal.

Overall Win and Lose

Rollo's military campaigns in France were marked by both successes and setbacks. While he achieved considerable victories in battle and amassed vast wealth and territory through his plundering raids, he also faced fierce opposition from the Frankish kings and their armies. Despite his prowess as a warrior, Rollo recognized the need for a more permanent settlement to secure his hold on the land and ensure the survival of his people.

Interesting Facts and Figures

- In 911, Rollo negotiated a historic treaty with King Charles the Simple of France, known as the Treaty of Saint-Clair-sur-Epte. According to the terms of the treaty, Rollo agreed to cease his raids and settle in the region of Normandy, which would henceforth be named after the Norsemen who had conquered it. In return, King Charles granted Rollo and his followers land and autonomy, effectively establishing the Duchy of Normandy as a buffer state between France and the Viking territories to the north.
- Rollo's descendants would go on to rule Normandy for generations, wielding power and influence throughout Europe and ultimately playing a key role in the Norman conquest of

England in 1066. Rollo's great-great-great-grandson, William the Conqueror, would become the first Norman king of England, cementing the legacy of the Viking chieftain who had founded the dynasty.
- Despite his reputation as a fearsome warrior and conqueror, Rollo was also known for his pragmatism and statesmanship. He recognized the value of diplomacy and negotiation in securing his objectives and was willing to compromise with his enemies when it served his interests. His willingness to adapt and evolve ensured the long-term survival and prosperity of the Norman people.

Death

Rollo died around the year 932, having lived to see the establishment of the Norman dynasty in France and the beginning of his descendants' rise to power and prominence in Europe. He was succeeded as ruler of Normandy by his son, William Longsword, who continued his father's legacy of expansion and consolidation.

In conclusion, Rollo of Normandy stands as a towering figure of the Viking Age, whose exploits and achievements helped to shape the course of European history. From humble beginnings as a Norse chieftain, he rose to become the founder of one of the most influential dynasties of the Middle Ages, leaving a lasting imprint on the lands and peoples of France and England. Rollo's legacy as a warrior, statesman, and pioneer of Norman civilization endures to this day, inspiring admiration and fascination among historians and enthusiasts of medieval history.

39

Rorke's Drift Heroes (United Kingdom)

The Battle of Rorke's Drift stands as one of the most celebrated engagements in British military history, showcasing the bravery, resilience, and camaraderie of a small band of soldiers faced with overwhelming odds. Taking place during the Anglo-Zulu War of 1879 in present-day South Africa, the defense of Rorke's Drift saw British forces holding off a determined assault by thousands of Zulu warriors, resulting in a remarkable victory that captured the imagination of the Victorian era and continues to inspire admiration and respect today.

Birth

The heroes of Rorke's Drift came from diverse backgrounds and regions of the British Empire, but they were united by their courage, loyalty, and sense of duty to their country. Many of them were regular soldiers serving in the British Army's 24th Regiment of Foot, while others were colonial troops or volunteers from various parts of the British Empire.

Early Life and Education

The soldiers who defended Rorke's Drift hailed from different walks of life, with varied experiences and backgrounds shaping their paths to military service. Some were born into military families and had been exposed to the rigors of army life from a young age, while others joined the military as a means of escaping poverty or seeking adventure overseas.

Wars

The Battle of Rorke's Drift occurred on January 22-23, 1879, during the Anglo-Zulu War, a conflict between the British Empire and the Zulu Kingdom in southern Africa. The battle was fought at a British supply depot and mission station called Rorke's Drift, located near the border between the British colony of Natal and the Zulu kingdom.

The engagement began when a large force of Zulu warriors, numbering around 4,000 strong, launched a surprise attack on the British garrison at Rorke's Drift, which was defended by approximately 140 British and colonial troops. Despite being heavily outnumbered, the defenders quickly rallied to their positions and prepared to repel the Zulu assault.

Overall Win and Lose

The defense of Rorke's Drift was a resounding success for the British Empire, as the small garrison managed to hold off repeated attacks by the Zulu warriors over two days. Despite facing overwhelming odds and sustaining heavy casualties, the defenders displayed remarkable courage, discipline, and resourcefulness, ultimately repelling the Zulu attackers and securing the strategic outpost.

Interesting Facts and Figures

- The Battle of Rorke's Drift was immortalized in the 1964 film "Zulu," which dramatized the events of the engagement and brought international attention to the heroism of the British soldiers who fought there. The film remains a classic of the war genre and has helped to ensure that the story of Rorke's Drift continues to be remembered and celebrated.
- Eleven Victoria Crosses, the highest award for gallantry in the British military, were awarded to the defenders of Rorke's Drift for their bravery and valor during the battle. This remains the largest number of Victoria Crosses ever awarded for a single

action in British military history, underscoring the extraordinary heroism displayed by the soldiers who defended the outpost.
- Despite their victory at Rorke's Drift, the British ultimately faced defeat in the broader conflict with the Zulu Kingdom, as evidenced by their disastrous defeat at the Battle of Isandlwana, which occurred on the same day as the defense of Rorke's Drift. The Battle of Isandlwana saw a British force of over 1,300 soldiers massacred by a Zulu army, highlighting the perils of underestimating one's enemy and the challenges of waging war in unfamiliar terrain.

Death

While the defenders of Rorke's Drift emerged victorious from the battle, their success came at a heavy cost. Twenty British and colonial troops were killed in action during the fighting, and another ten were wounded. The Zulu casualties were estimated to be over 500 warriors killed or wounded, highlighting the ferocity and intensity of the engagement.

In conclusion, the heroes of Rorke's Drift demonstrated the courage, determination, and sacrifice that have come to symbolize the best qualities of the British military tradition. Their heroic stand against overwhelming odds remains a source of inspiration and pride for generations of soldiers and civilians alike, serving as a reminder of the power of courage, camaraderie, and resilience in the face of adversity.

40

Saigō Takamori (Japan)

Saigō Takamori, often referred to as the last samurai, was a prominent Japanese statesman and military leader who played a pivotal role in the overthrow of the Tokugawa shogunate and the restoration of imperial rule in Japan. Born into a samurai family in the Satsuma domain (present-day Kagoshima Prefecture), Saigō rose to prominence as a champion of traditional values and a fierce advocate for the preservation of samurai culture in the face of modernization and Western influence. His life and legacy embody the complex transition of Japan from feudal isolation to modernization in the late 19th century.

Birth

Saigō Takamori was born on January 23, 1828, in the village of Kajiya in the Satsuma domain, located on the southern island of Kyushu, Japan. He was born into a samurai family of lower rank, but his exceptional intelligence, leadership qualities, and martial prowess quickly distinguished him from his peers. From a young age, Saigō was immersed in the traditions of bushido, the samurai code of honor and loyalty, which would shape his character and guide his actions throughout his life.

Early Life and Education

As a young samurai, Saigō received a rigorous education in the martial arts, literature, and Confucian philosophy, as well as training in military strategy and tactics. He distinguished himself as a skilled swordsman and strategist, earning the respect and admiration of his superiors and peers. Saigō's early experiences in the Satsuma domain instilled in him a deep sense of loyalty to his lord and a commitment to the preservation of samurai values in the face of external threats.

Wars

Saigō Takamori's military career was marked by his participation in several key conflicts that shaped the course of Japanese history during the turbulent years of the Bakumatsu period (1853-1868) when Japan faced increasing pressure from Western powers to open its borders to foreign trade and diplomacy.

One of the most significant conflicts in which Saigō played a leading role was the Boshin War (1868-1869), a civil war between forces loyal to the Tokugawa shogunate and those supporting the imperial court. As a key leader of the Satsuma domain's forces, Saigō played a central role in the overthrow of the shogunate and the restoration of Emperor Meiji to supreme political power, marking the beginning of Japan's modern era.

Overall Win and Lose

Saigō Takamori's role in the Boshin War and the subsequent Meiji Restoration was instrumental in shaping the course of Japanese history and laying the foundations for Japan's rapid modernization and industrialization in the late 19th and early 20th centuries. Despite his success in overthrowing the Tokugawa shogunate and restoring imperial rule, Saigō's later years were marked by conflict and disillusionment as he found himself increasingly at odds with the policies of the Meiji government.

Interesting Facts and Figures

- Saigō Takamori is often remembered for his principled opposition to the rapid modernization and Westernization of Japan that followed the Meiji Restoration. He was a staunch advocate for the preservation of traditional Japanese values and institutions, including the samurai class, which he believed were essential to the nation's identity and unity. Saigō's adherence to these

principles earned him the admiration of many Japanese people, who saw him as a symbol of the samurai spirit and the virtues of bushido.
- Despite his reservations about the direction of the Meiji government, Saigō initially served as a prominent figure in the new administration, holding positions of authority and influence within the imperial court. However, he grew increasingly disillusioned with the government's policies, particularly its treatment of former samurai and its handling of foreign affairs.
- In 1873, Saigō resigned from his government positions and returned to his native Satsuma domain, where he founded a private military school and continued to advocate for samurai rights and autonomy. His efforts to maintain the samurai way of life and resist the encroachment of Western influence ultimately led to his involvement in a rebellion against the Meiji government known as the Satsuma Rebellion.

Death

The Satsuma Rebellion, also known as the Seinan War, erupted in 1877 when Saigō and his followers rose against the Meiji government in a last stand for samurai honor and autonomy. Despite initial successes, including the capture of several key cities in Kyushu, Saigō's forces were ultimately overwhelmed by the superior firepower and resources of the imperial army.

Saigō Takamori died on September 24, 1877, during the final battle of the Satsuma Rebellion, known as the Battle of Shiroyama. According to legend, Saigō committed seppuku, the ritual suicide of a samurai, upon being wounded in battle. His death marked the end of an era in Japanese history and the final stand of the samurai class against the tide of modernization and change.

In conclusion, Saigō Takamori was a pivotal figure in the transition of Japan from feudal isolation to modernization in the late 19th century. His unwavering commitment to samurai values and his role in overthrowing the Tokugawa shogunate left an indelible mark on Japanese history and culture, inspiring generations of Japanese people to honor the traditions of bushido and the legacy of the samurai. Despite his ultimate defeat in the Satsuma Rebellion, Saigō's legacy as the last samurai endures as a symbol of courage, honor, and loyalty in the face of adversity.

41

Saladin (Egypt/Syria)

Saladin, known in Arabic as Salah ad-Din Yusuf ibn Ayyub, was a towering figure in medieval Islamic history, revered as a brilliant military commander, statesman, and Islamic leader. Born into a Kurdish family in Tikrit, Iraq, Saladin rose to prominence during the tumultuous years of the Crusades, eventually uniting the Muslim world and achieving remarkable military successes against the Christian forces of the Crusader states. His legacy as a chivalrous and merciful ruler, as well as his role in reclaiming Jerusalem for Islam, endures to this day.

Birth

Saladin was born in 1137 in the town of Tikrit, located on the banks of the Tigris River in present-day Iraq. He was born into a Sunni Muslim Kurdish family of noble descent, with his father, Najm ad-Din Ayyub, serving as a military commander in the service of the Zengid dynasty, rulers of Mosul and Aleppo.

Early Life and Education

Little is known about Saladin's early life and education, but it is believed that he received training in martial arts, horsemanship, and military strategy from an early age. He also received a comprehensive education in Islamic theology, jurisprudence, and literature, as befitting his status as a member of the ruling elite.

Wars

Saladin's military career began in earnest in the 1160s, when he served as a lieutenant under his uncle Shirkuh, a prominent military commander in the service of the Zengid dynasty. Together, they played a key role in the Zengid conquest of Egypt in 1169, overthrowing the Fatimid caliphate and establishing the Ayyubid dynasty, with Saladin appointed as vizier, or chief minister, of Egypt.

However, Saladin's ambitions extended far beyond Egypt, and he soon set his sights on the liberation of Jerusalem from the Crusader states, which had been established by European Christians in the wake of the First Crusade in 1099. Throughout his military campaigns in the Levant, Saladin achieved remarkable successes against the Crusaders, eventually leading to the recapture of Jerusalem in 1187.

Overall Win and Lose

Saladin's military campaigns against the Crusader states were marked by both victories and setbacks. While he succeeded in uniting the Muslim world and reclaiming significant territories from the Crusaders, including Jerusalem, his efforts to establish a lasting Muslim empire in the Levant ultimately fell short. Despite his failure to achieve all of his objectives, Saladin's legacy as a hero of Islam and a symbol of resistance to foreign domination endures to this day.

Interesting Facts and Figures

- Saladin's reputation as a chivalrous and magnanimous ruler earned him the admiration of his enemies as well as his allies. Following his capture of Jerusalem in 1187, Saladin famously demonstrated his mercy and generosity by allowing the Christian inhabitants to leave the city unharmed and offering them safe passage to Christian territory. His actions earned him praise from European chroniclers and cemented his reputation as a paragon of Islamic virtue and honor.
- Saladin's military campaigns against the Crusaders were marked by his strategic brilliance and tactical acumen. He employed a combination of military force, diplomacy, and propaganda to

weaken the Crusader states and rally support from the Muslim world. His victories at the Battle of Hattin in 1187 and the subsequent siege of Jerusalem were decisive turning points in the struggle for control of the Holy Land.
- Despite his successes on the battlefield, Saladin faced numerous challenges in maintaining the unity of the Muslim world and securing his hold on the territories he had conquered. Internal rivalries, shifting alliances, and external threats from both the Crusaders and the Mongols posed constant challenges to his authority and stability.

Death

Saladin died on March 4, 1193, in Damascus, Syria, at the age of 55. He was buried in a mausoleum near the Umayyad Mosque in Damascus, where his tomb remains a revered pilgrimage site for Muslims to this day. Saladin's death marked the end of an era in Islamic history and the beginning of a period of decline for the Ayyubid dynasty, which would eventually succumb to internal strife and external pressures.

In conclusion, Saladin was a towering figure in medieval Islamic history, whose military exploits, statesmanship, and chivalry continue to inspire admiration and respect centuries after his death. His role in uniting the Muslim world, reclaiming Jerusalem from the Crusaders, and establishing a legacy of tolerance and justice has left an indelible mark on the collective memory of Muslims around the world. As a symbol of Islamic resistance and unity, Saladin remains a source of pride and inspiration for generations of Muslims seeking to uphold the values of justice, compassion, and dignity.

42

Scipio Africanus (Rome)

Scipio Africanus, also known as Publius Cornelius Scipio Africanus, was one of ancient Rome's most illustrious military leaders and statesmen. Born into a prominent Roman family during the height of the Roman Republic, Scipio rose to prominence through his military exploits and diplomatic skills. He is best known for his pivotal role in defeating the Carthaginian general Hannibal during the Second Punic War, thereby securing Rome's dominance in the Mediterranean world.

Birth

Scipio Africanus was born in 236 BCE into the noble Cornelii family, one of the most distinguished patrician families in ancient Rome. His birthplace is believed to be Rome itself, although the exact details of his early life and upbringing are not well-documented. From a young age, Scipio was immersed in the traditions of the Roman aristocracy and received a comprehensive education in literature, philosophy, and military strategy.

Early Life and Education

As a member of the Cornelii family, Scipio enjoyed privileges and opportunities that were unavailable to the common citizens of Rome. He received a rigorous education in martial arts, literature, and oratory, as well as training in the customs and traditions of Roman society. His upbringing instilled in him a strong sense of duty, honor, and patriotism, as well as a keen ambition to distinguish himself in the service of the Roman state.

Wars

Scipio Africanus's military career began in earnest during the Second Punic War (218-201 BCE), a conflict between Rome and Carthage for control of the western Mediterranean. In 218 BCE, Hannibal, the Carthaginian general, famously crossed the Alps with his army and launched a devastating invasion of Italy, catching the Romans off guard and inflicting a series of crushing defeats on them.

Despite these setbacks, Scipio remained undaunted and quickly emerged as one of Rome's most promising young commanders. In 211 BCE, he was appointed as consul and given command of Roman forces in Spain, where he achieved a series of decisive victories against Carthaginian forces under the command of Hannibal's brother, Hasdrubal. Scipio's successes in Spain earned him the nickname "Africanus," in recognition of his ambitions to take the fight to Carthage itself.

Overall Win and Lose

Scipio Africanus's greatest triumph came in 202 BCE, when he decisively defeated Hannibal at the Battle of Zama, near Carthage. By employing innovative tactics and exploiting Hannibal's weaknesses, Scipio managed to outmaneuver and outmaneuver the Carthaginian army, securing a resounding victory for Rome and bringing an end to the Second Punic War. His victory at Zama established Rome as the dominant power in the western Mediterranean and marked the beginning of the decline of Carthage as a major political and military force.

Interesting Facts and Figures

- Scipio Africanus was renowned not only for his military prowess but also for his statesmanship and diplomacy. Following his victory over Hannibal, he played a key role in negotiating the terms of peace with Carthage, which resulted in a favorable settlement for Rome and ensured its dominance in the Mediterranean world. Scipio's statesmanship and vision helped to shape the

course of Roman history and establish Rome as a superpower in the ancient world.
- In addition to his military and political achievements, Scipio Africanus was also known for his cultural and intellectual interests. He was a patron of the arts and sciences, and he played a significant role in promoting Greek culture and learning in Rome. He was also a prolific writer and historian, and his writings on military strategy and tactics had a lasting influence on subsequent generations of military leaders.
- Despite his many successes, Scipio Africanus's career was not without controversy. In later years, he became embroiled in political disputes and accusations of corruption, which tarnished his reputation and led to his eventual retirement from public life. Nevertheless, his legacy as one of Rome's greatest generals and statesmen endured long after his death.

Death

Scipio Africanus died in 183 BCE at the age of 53, having retired from public life and withdrawn to his estate in Campania. His death marked the end of an era in Roman history and the passing of one of Rome's most illustrious and influential figures. Despite the controversies and challenges he faced during his lifetime, Scipio Africanus's legacy as a hero of Rome and a symbol of its military and political greatness endures to this day.

In conclusion, Scipio Africanus was a towering figure in ancient Roman history, whose military exploits, statesmanship, and cultural achievements helped to shape the course of the Roman Republic and establish Rome as a dominant power in the Mediterranean world. His victory over Hannibal at the Battle of Zama remains one of the most celebrated achievements in military history, and his legacy as a patriot, leader, and visionary leader continues to inspire admiration and respect centuries after his death.

43

Shaka Zulu (Zulu Kingdom)

Shaka Zulu, one of Africa's most iconic and enigmatic figures, was a military genius and statesman who transformed the Zulu tribe into a formidable military power and laid the foundations for the Zulu Kingdom in southern Africa. Born in the early 19th century, Shaka rose to prominence through his innovative military tactics, organizational reforms, and charismatic leadership. His legacy as a visionary ruler and military strategist endures to this day, shaping the course of Zulu history and inspiring generations of Africans.

Birth

Shaka Zulu was born in 1787 in the small chiefdom of the Zulu tribe, located in present-day KwaZulu-Natal province, South Africa. He was the son of Chief Senzangakhona kaJama, a minor chief in the region, and Nandi, a woman of the Langeni clan. Shaka's birth was marred by controversy and hardship, as his mother faced ostracism and rejection from her community due to the circumstances of his conception.

Early Life and Education

Shaka's early years were marked by adversity and struggle, as he faced discrimination and rejection from his peers due to his illegitimate birth. Despite these challenges, Shaka displayed remarkable intelligence, athleticism, and martial prowess from a young age, earning him the respect and admiration of his father's warriors. He received a rudimentary education in Zulu customs, traditions, and warfare, as well as training in the use of weapons such as the spear and shield.

Wars

Shaka's rise to power began in the early 19th century when he assumed leadership of the Zulu tribe following his father's death. Determined to unify and strengthen his people, Shaka embarked on a series of military campaigns aimed at expanding the boundaries of the Zulu kingdom and consolidating his control over neighboring chiefdoms.

One of Shaka's most significant military innovations was the formation of the impi, a highly disciplined and mobile fighting force composed of young Zulu warriors armed with short stabbing spears known as iklwa. Under Shaka's leadership, the Zulu impi became a formidable military machine, capable of overwhelming larger and more established adversaries through speed, agility, and sheer ferocity.

Overall Win and Lose

Shaka Zulu's military campaigns were marked by both victories and defeats, but his overall impact on southern African history was profound. By the time of his death in 1828, Shaka had succeeded in creating a centralized Zulu state with a powerful army and a network of allied chiefdoms. His conquests transformed the political landscape of southern Africa and laid the foundations for the emergence of the Zulu Kingdom as a dominant regional power.

Interesting Facts and Figures

- Shaka Zulu's military innovations revolutionized the art of warfare in southern Africa and had a lasting impact on the region's history. His introduction of the "bull horn" formation, a tactical maneuver that involved encircling and enveloping the enemy, proved devastatingly effective against traditional African armies and enabled the Zulu impi to achieve numerous victories on the battlefield.
- Despite his reputation as a fearsome warrior and ruthless leader, Shaka was also known for his visionary leadership and

administrative reforms. He implemented a system of centralized authority and governance within the Zulu kingdom, creating a hierarchy of military ranks and establishing a network of military outposts and administrative centers throughout his domain.
- Shaka's reign as king of the Zulu tribe was not without controversy, and his methods of rule were often brutal and uncompromising. He was known for his ruthless suppression of dissent and his willingness to resort to violence to maintain his authority. Nevertheless, Shaka's achievements as a military leader and nation-builder continue to command respect and admiration among historians and scholars.

Death

Shaka Zulu met a tragic end in 1828 when he was assassinated by his half-brothers, Dingane and Mhlangana, who conspired to overthrow him and seize power for themselves. His death marked the end of an era in Zulu history and plunged the kingdom into a period of instability and conflict. Despite his untimely demise, Shaka's legacy as a visionary leader and military genius endures to this day, shaping the identity and heritage of the Zulu people and inspiring generations of Africans.

In conclusion, Shaka Zulu stands as one of Africa's most iconic and influential figures, whose military prowess, organizational reforms, and charismatic leadership transformed the Zulu tribe into a powerful and respected kingdom. His legacy as a visionary ruler and nation-builder continues to resonate in southern Africa, where he is celebrated as a hero and a symbol of Zulu pride and resilience.

44

Simon Bolivar (Venezuela/Gran Colombia)

Simon Bolivar, often referred to as the "Liberator," was a towering figure in the struggle for independence in Latin America during the early 19th century. Born into a wealthy aristocratic family in Venezuela, Bolivar emerged as a charismatic leader and visionary statesman who played a central role in liberating much of South America from Spanish colonial rule. His legacy as a champion of freedom, democracy, and pan-American unity continues to resonate across the region to this day.

Birth

Simon Bolivar was born on July 24, 1783, in Caracas, Venezuela, which was then part of the Spanish colonial empire. He was born into a privileged family of Spanish descent, with ancestral ties to the highest echelons of Venezuelan society. Bolivar's upbringing was marked by wealth and privilege, but also by tragedy, as he lost both of his parents at a young age.

Early Life and Education

Bolivar's early years were shaped by the political and social upheaval of the late 18th century, as revolutionary ideas of liberty and equality spread throughout Latin America and Europe. Despite his privileged upbringing, Bolivar became deeply influenced by Enlightenment ideals and the democratic revolutions taking place in North America and

Europe. He received a classical education in literature, philosophy, and politics, which laid the foundation for his future as a revolutionary leader.

Wars

Simon Bolivar's revolutionary career began in earnest in 1810 when he joined the movement for Venezuelan independence from Spanish rule. Inspired by the example of the United States and other revolutionary movements in Latin America, Bolivar quickly emerged as a leading figure in the struggle for independence, rallying support from across the region and organizing a series of military campaigns against Spanish forces.

One of Bolivar's most notable military achievements came in 1813 when he led a daring campaign known as the "Admirable Campaign" to liberate Venezuela from Spanish control. Despite initial successes, Bolivar's forces were ultimately defeated by Spanish loyalists, forcing him into exile in neighboring Colombia. Undeterred by this setback, Bolivar continued his fight for independence, rallying support from across South America and forging alliances with other revolutionary leaders.

Overall Win and Lose

Simon Bolivar's military campaigns were marked by both victories and defeats, but his overall impact on the struggle for independence in Latin America was profound. By the time of his death in 1830, Bolivar had succeeded in liberating much of South America from Spanish colonial rule, including present-day Venezuela, Colombia, Ecuador, Peru, and Bolivia. His vision of a united and independent South America, known as "Gran Colombia," laid the groundwork for the emergence of modern nation-states in the region.

Interesting Facts and Figures

- Simon Bolivar was not only a military leader but also a visionary statesman and political philosopher. He played a central role in drafting constitutions and establishing republican governments in the newly liberated nations of Latin America, advocating for principles of democracy, equality, and social justice. Bolivar's writings on politics and governance, including his "Cartagena Manifesto" and "Letter from Jamaica," remain influential texts in Latin American history.

- Bolivar's efforts to unite South America under a single federation, known as Gran Colombia, ultimately proved unsuccessful due to regional rivalries and political divisions. Despite his best efforts to promote unity and cooperation among the newly independent nations, Gran Colombia dissolved into separate republics shortly after his death. Nevertheless, Bolivar's dream of a united South America remains a powerful symbol of pan-American solidarity and aspiration.

- Bolivar's legacy as a revolutionary hero and champion of liberty has earned him widespread acclaim and reverence throughout Latin America. His image adorns currency, monuments, and public spaces across the region, and his name is synonymous with the struggle for independence and national identity. Bolivar's birthday, July 24th, is celebrated as a national holiday in Venezuela and other countries, commemorating his enduring legacy as the "Liberator" of South America.

Death

Simon Bolivar died on December 17, 1830, at the age of 47, in Santa Marta, Colombia. His death marked the end of an era in Latin American history and the passing of one of the region's most iconic and influential figures. Bolivar's legacy as a champion of freedom, democracy, and pan-American unity continues to inspire generations of Latin Americans, who look to him as a symbol of hope, resilience, and liberation.

In conclusion, Simon Bolivar stands as one of Latin America's most revered and celebrated heroes, whose vision of independence, democracy, and pan-American unity continues to shape the region's identity and aspirations. His tireless efforts to liberate South America from

Spanish colonial rule and establish republican governments founded on principles of freedom and equality have left an indelible mark on the history and culture of the continent. As the "Liberator" of South America, Bolivar's legacy endures as a source of inspiration and pride for generations to come.

45

Sitting Bull (Lakota Sioux)

Sitting Bull, a legendary figure among the Lakota Sioux and a prominent leader in the resistance against American encroachment on Native American lands, emerged as a symbol of indigenous resilience and defiance in the face of colonial expansion. Born into the Hunkpapa Lakota tribe in present-day South Dakota, Sitting Bull rose to prominence as a spiritual leader, warrior, and diplomat during a period of profound upheaval and conflict in the American West. His steadfast resistance to U.S. government policies and his role in the Battle of the Little Bighorn cemented his status as one of the most iconic figures in Native American history.

Birth

Sitting Bull was born in 1831 near the Grand River in present-day South Dakota, within the territory of the Hunkpapa Lakota Sioux tribe. He was born into the Hunkpapa band of the Lakota, a division of the Sioux people known for their fierce independence and warrior tradition. From a young age, Sitting Bull displayed leadership qualities and a deep connection to Lakota spiritual beliefs and traditions.

Early Life and Education

As a member of the Hunkpapa Lakota, Sitting Bull grew up immersed in the rich cultural heritage and traditions of his people. He received a traditional Lakota education, learning the skills of hunting, horseback riding, and warfare from his elders. He also underwent spiritual training and initiation rites, which instilled in him a profound sense of reverence for the natural world and the spiritual forces that governed it.

Wars

Sitting Bull's life and legacy are closely intertwined with the struggle of the Lakota Sioux to defend their ancestral lands and way of life against encroachment by white settlers and the U.S. government. Throughout the 19th century, tensions between Native American tribes and the expanding United States led to a series of conflicts and wars, as the federal government sought to forcibly remove indigenous peoples from their homelands and open up the West to settlement and exploitation.

One of the most significant battles in which Sitting Bull played a central role was the Battle of the Little Bighorn in 1876. In this dramatic confrontation, Sitting Bull allied with other Lakota Sioux leaders, such as Crazy Horse and Gall, to repel an incursion by U.S. Army forces led by General George Armstrong Custer. The battle resulted in a stunning victory for the Lakota Sioux and their allies, but it also brought intensified military pressure from the U.S. government.

Overall Win and Lose

Sitting Bull's resistance to American expansionism was ultimately unsuccessful in preventing the subjugation and displacement of the Lakota Sioux from their ancestral lands. Following the defeat of Custer at the Battle of the Little Bighorn, the U.S. government intensified its efforts to suppress Lakota resistance and compel them to relocate to reservations. In 1881, Sitting Bull surrendered to U.S. authorities and was confined to the Standing Rock Indian Reservation in present-day North Dakota.

Interesting Facts and Figures

- Sitting Bull was not only a military leader but also a spiritual leader and visionary figure within the Lakota Sioux community. He was revered as a holy man and a prophet, believed to possess supernatural powers and insights into the future. His visions and

prophecies played a crucial role in guiding the actions and decisions of the Lakota people during a time of great uncertainty and upheaval.
- Sitting Bull's reputation as a fierce and uncompromising opponent of white encroachment on Native American lands made him a symbol of resistance and defiance throughout the American West. He was admired by many of his contemporaries for his courage, tenacity, and unwavering commitment to the preservation of Lakota sovereignty and cultural identity.
- Sitting Bull's fame and influence extended beyond the borders of the United States, as he became a symbol of indigenous resistance and solidarity around the world. He was celebrated as a hero and freedom fighter by indigenous peoples in other countries, who saw in him a beacon of hope and inspiration in their struggles against colonialism and oppression.

Death

Sitting Bull's life came to a tragic end on December 15, 1890, when he was killed during a confrontation with Indian agency police on the Standing Rock Reservation. The circumstances surrounding his death remain the subject of controversy and debate, but his legacy as a champion of indigenous rights and sovereignty continues to resonate among Native American communities and activists to this day.

In conclusion, Sitting Bull occupies a central place in the pantheon of Native American heroes and leaders, revered for his courage, wisdom, and indomitable spirit in the face of overwhelming odds. His legacy as a symbol of indigenous resistance and resilience endures as a powerful reminder of the ongoing struggle for justice and equality in the Americas and beyond. Sitting Bull's life and achievements serve as an inspiration to future generations of Native Americans and all those who champion the cause of social justice and human rights.

46

Spartacus (Thrace)

Spartacus, a figure of myth and legend, rose from obscurity to lead one of the most famous slave uprisings in history. Born into slavery in the Roman province of Thrace, Spartacus defied the odds to become a symbol of resistance against the oppressive Roman Empire. His story of courage, determination, and defiance has captivated generations and continues to inspire movements for freedom and equality worldwide.

Birth

Spartacus was born around 111 BCE in Thrace, a region located in present-day Bulgaria, Greece, and Turkey. Little is known about his early life, but it is believed that he was born into slavery, a common fate for many inhabitants of the region under Roman rule. Like many enslaved people of his time, Spartacus likely endured harsh treatment and exploitation at the hands of his Roman masters.

Early Life and Education

As a slave in the Roman Empire, Spartacus would have received little to no formal education. Instead, he would have been trained in manual labor and forced to perform grueling tasks under the supervision of his masters. Despite the hardships he endured, Spartacus possessed a keen intellect and a strong sense of justice, qualities that would later shape his destiny as a leader of men.

Wars

Spartacus's transformation from a slave to a revolutionary leader began in 73 BCE when he escaped from a gladiatorial training school in Capua, along with a group of fellow slaves. Determined to win their freedom, Spartacus and his comrades seized weapons and equipment from their captors and embarked on a daring campaign of rebellion against the Roman authorities.

What began as a small-scale uprising soon grew into a full-fledged rebellion, as Spartacus's ranks swelled with other disaffected slaves and free individuals from across Italy. Spartacus proved to be a skilled tactician and military leader, leading his followers in a series of audacious raids and skirmishes against Roman forces.

Overall Win and Lose

Despite his military prowess and the initial success of his rebellion, Spartacus ultimately met a tragic end at the Battle of the Siler River in 71 BCE. Facing overwhelming numbers and superior discipline, Spartacus and his forces were defeated by the Roman legions under the command of Marcus Licinius Crassus. Spartacus himself was killed in battle, and his body was never recovered.

Interesting Facts and Figures

- One of the most remarkable aspects of Spartacus's rebellion was its ability to unite people from diverse backgrounds and social classes under a common cause. Spartacus's army included not only enslaved people but also free individuals, deserters from the Roman army, and even some Roman citizens who had been drawn to his banner by the promise of freedom and adventure.
- Spartacus's rebellion struck fear into the hearts of Rome's ruling elite, who viewed him as a dangerous subversive and a threat to their power and privilege. The Senate dispatched several armies to crush the rebellion, but Spartacus repeatedly outmaneuvered and defeated them, earning a reputation as a formidable opponent and a symbol of hope for the oppressed.

- Spartacus's legacy as a symbol of resistance and liberation has endured for centuries, inspiring countless works of literature, art, and film. His story has been immortalized in numerous plays, novels, and movies, including the iconic film "Spartacus" directed by Stanley Kubrick and starring Kirk Douglas in the title role.

Death

Spartacus met his end on the battlefield, fighting bravely alongside his fellow rebels against overwhelming odds. Although his rebellion ultimately failed to achieve its objectives, Spartacus's courage, determination, and sacrifice left an indelible mark on history and inspired countless generations to come.

In conclusion, Spartacus's story is a testament to the power of the human spirit to overcome oppression and injustice. Born into slavery, Spartacus defied the odds to become a symbol of resistance and liberation, inspiring millions around the world to stand up against tyranny and fight for their freedom. Though his rebellion was ultimately crushed by the might of the Roman Empire, Spartacus's legacy lives on as a shining example of courage, defiance, and the eternal struggle for justice.

Subutai (Mongolia)

Subutai, often referred to as the "Greatest General of the Mongol Empire," was a brilliant military strategist and one of the most influential figures in world history. Born into the Mongol tribes of Central Asia, Subutai rose through the ranks to become a trusted advisor and close confidant of Genghis Khan, the founder of the Mongol Empire. Renowned for his tactical genius, strategic vision, and relentless pursuit of victory, Subutai played a pivotal role in expanding the Mongol Empire to its greatest extent and shaping the course of world events during the 13th century.

Birth

Subutai was born around 1175 in the Mongol heartland of Central Asia, possibly in what is now present-day Mongolia. Little is known about his early life or family background, but he likely grew up in a nomadic lifestyle typical of the Mongol tribes, honing his skills in horseback riding, archery, and warfare from a young age.

Early Life and Education

As a member of the Mongol tribes, Subutai would have received a practical education in the arts of war and survival from his elders and mentors. He would have learned the traditional skills of hunting, herding, and horsemanship that were essential for life on the Central Asian steppes, as well as the tactics and strategies of Mongol warfare that would later propel him to greatness.

Wars

Subutai's rise to prominence came during the early years of the Mongol conquests under Genghis Khan. Recognizing his exceptional talents as a military commander, Genghis Khan appointed Subutai to key positions of leadership within the Mongol army, where he quickly distinguished himself in battle.

One of Subutai's most notable campaigns was the invasion of the Khwarezmian Empire in the early 13th century. Leading a vast army of Mongol warriors, Subutai launched a lightning-fast campaign of conquest across Central Asia, defeating the forces of the Khwarezmian Shah and bringing the entire region under Mongol control. The speed, coordination, and ferocity of Subutai's attacks earned him a fearsome reputation among his enemies and established him as one of the pre-eminent military leaders of his time.

Overall Win and Lose

Subutai's military campaigns were marked by overwhelming success and few defeats. Under his leadership, the Mongol Empire expanded rapidly, conquering vast territories from China to Eastern Europe and establishing the largest contiguous land empire in history. Subutai's strategic brilliance, innovative tactics, and mastery of logistics played a crucial role in the Mongols' ability to overcome formidable opponents and conquer seemingly impregnable fortresses.

Interesting Facts and Figures

- Subutai's military campaigns took him to the farthest reaches of Asia and Europe, where he faced a wide array of adversaries, from the fortified cities of China to the knights of Western Europe. His ability to adapt his tactics and strategies to suit the terrain and the capabilities of his enemies made him a formidable foe and a master of asymmetric warfare.
- Subutai was a pioneer in the use of psychological warfare and deception tactics to demoralize and confuse his opponents. He often employed feints, ambushes, and false retreats to lure enemy

forces into vulnerable positions and then strike with devastating force when they least expected it. His ability to outmaneuver and outthink his adversaries earned him the nickname "the Invincible Subutai" among his Mongol comrades.
- Subutai's military genius extended beyond the battlefield to the realm of logistics and supply. He was a master of organization and planning, able to coordinate the movements of vast armies across thousands of miles of hostile territory with remarkable efficiency. His ability to keep his troops well-fed, well-equipped, and well-supplied was a key factor in the success of the Mongol conquests.

Death

Subutai's exact date and circumstances of death are uncertain, but he is believed to have died around 1248, possibly from natural causes or old age. His death marked the passing of one of the greatest military minds in history, leaving behind a legacy of conquest and achievement that would shape the course of world events for centuries to come.

In conclusion, Subutai's legacy as one of the greatest military commanders of all time is a testament to the power of strategic thinking, innovation, and determination. His achievements on the battlefield helped to forge the largest empire in history and reshape the geopolitical landscape of Asia and Europe. As a master tactician and visionary leader, Subutai's influence continues to be felt to this day, inspiring future generations of military leaders and scholars alike.

48

Sun Tzu (China)

Sun Tzu, the legendary Chinese military strategist and philosopher, is renowned for his seminal work "The Art of War," which has profoundly influenced military tactics, strategy, and leadership across the globe for over two millennia. Born in ancient China during a time of political turmoil and interstate conflict, Sun Tzu's teachings on warfare and statecraft remain as relevant today as they were in his own time. His profound insights into strategy, deception, and leadership continue to inspire leaders in fields beyond the military, including business, politics, and sports.

Birth

Sun Tzu, also known by his birth name Sun Wu, was born in the state of Qi, in what is now present-day Shandong province, China, around 544 BCE. Little is known about his early life, including details about his family background or upbringing. However, his enduring legacy as a military strategist and philosopher suggests that he received a comprehensive education in the arts of war and statecraft from a young age.

Early Life and Education

As a young man, Sun Tzu likely received a classical education typical of the Chinese elite of his time, which would have included studies in literature, philosophy, and military strategy. He may have also received practical training in martial arts and military tactics, as warfare was a central aspect of life in ancient China during the Warring States period.

Wars

Sun Tzu's most enduring contribution to military history is his timeless treatise "The Art of War," which he is believed to have composed during the late Spring and Autumn period (around the 5th century BCE). "The Art of War" is a comprehensive guide to strategy, tactics, and leadership on the battlefield, offering practical advice on everything from the selection of terrain and the deployment of troops to the use of espionage and psychological warfare.

Overall Win and Lose

Sun Tzu's teachings on warfare and strategy have had a profound and lasting impact on military theory and practice around the world. His emphasis on the importance of understanding one's strengths and weaknesses, exploiting the vulnerabilities of one's opponents, and adapting to changing circumstances remains as relevant today as it was in ancient China.

Interesting Facts and Figures

- One of the most famous anecdotes about Sun Tzu involves his demonstration of his military prowess to the King of Wu, who was skeptical of his abilities. In response, Sun Tzu was said to have trained the king's concubines in the art of warfare, using them to demonstrate his principles of discipline, leadership, and strategy. Impressed by the results, the king appointed Sun Tzu as his chief military advisor.
- Sun Tzu's teachings on strategy and leadership extend beyond the battlefield to the realm of politics, diplomacy, and business. Many of his principles, such as the importance of deception, the value of intelligence gathering, and the necessity of adaptability, have been applied with great success in fields beyond the military, including business management, negotiation, and competitive sports.

Death

The exact details of Sun Tzu's death are unknown, but he is believed to have passed away around 496 BCE, possibly in the state of Wu, where he served as a military advisor to the king. Despite the passage of centuries, Sun Tzu's legacy as one of history's greatest military strategists and philosophers endures, inspiring leaders and warriors around the world to this day.

In conclusion, Sun Tzu's enduring legacy as a military strategist and philosopher is a testament to the timeless wisdom of his teachings. His insights into strategy, leadership, and the nature of conflict have transcended the boundaries of time and culture, inspiring generations of leaders and warriors to strive for excellence and achieve victory in the face of adversity. As one of the most influential figures in military history, Sun Tzu's teachings continue to shape the way we think about warfare, leadership, and the pursuit of success.

49

Suvorov (Russia)

Alexander Vasilyevich Suvorov, commonly known as Suvorov, was one of Russia's greatest military commanders and a prominent figure in European military history. Born into a noble family in Russia in 1729, Suvorov rose through the ranks of the Russian army to become renowned for his strategic brilliance, tactical innovation, and unwavering dedication to the art of war. His military campaigns, marked by daring maneuvers and decisive victories, earned him a reputation as one of the most successful and respected generals of his time.

Birth

Alexander Suvorov was born on November 24, 1729, in Moscow, Russia. He was the son of Vasily Suvorov, a general-in-chief in the Russian army, and Anna Suvorova, a member of the noble Rostovtsev family. From an early age, Suvorov displayed a keen interest in military affairs and received a rigorous education in martial arts, tactics, and strategy.

Early Life and Education

Suvorov's upbringing was deeply influenced by his family's military background and the prevailing ethos of service to the Russian state. He received a comprehensive education that included training in horsemanship, swordsmanship, and military theory, as well as studies in mathematics, geography, and history. His early experiences instilled in him a sense of duty, discipline, and patriotism that would shape his character and career.

Wars

Suvorov's military career began in earnest in the 1740s when he entered the Russian army as a cadet. He quickly distinguished himself in battle, displaying courage, leadership, and tactical acumen beyond his years. Throughout his career, Suvorov participated in numerous campaigns and military operations, earning a reputation for his daring maneuvers, decisive victories, and unwavering commitment to his soldiers.

One of Suvorov's most famous campaigns was his Italian and Swiss expedition of 1799 during the War of the Second Coalition. Leading a Russian army against French forces in northern Italy, Suvorov achieved a series of stunning victories, including the Battle of Cassano, the Battle of Trebbia, and the Battle of Novi. His brilliant tactics and aggressive leadership earned him the admiration of his troops and the respect of his enemies.

Overall Win and Lose

Throughout his military career, Suvorov demonstrated an uncanny ability to achieve victory against superior odds through a combination of strategic insight, tactical innovation, and bold leadership. His campaigns were marked by daring maneuvers, lightning-fast marches, and surprise attacks that often caught his adversaries off guard and led to decisive victories.

However, Suvorov's military successes were not without their setbacks. Despite his brilliance as a commander, he faced numerous challenges and obstacles, including logistical difficulties, political intrigues, and rivalries within the Russian court. Nevertheless, Suvorov's resilience, determination, and unwavering commitment to his soldiers enabled him to overcome these challenges and emerge victorious on the battlefield.

Interesting Facts and Figures

- Suvorov's military career spanned nearly five decades and encompassed numerous campaigns and battles across Europe and Asia. He fought in the Russo-Turkish Wars, the Seven Years' War, the War of the Bavarian Succession, and the War of the Second Coalition, among others.
- Suvorov was known for his strict discipline and Spartan lifestyle, which he believed were essential for maintaining the morale and effectiveness of his troops. He famously led his soldiers by example, sharing their hardships and enduring the same privations and dangers on the battlefield.
- Suvorov was a master of unconventional warfare and psychological tactics, often using deception, surprise, and maneuver to outwit and outmaneuver his adversaries. His famous motto, "Victory is gained not by numbers, but by knowing how to use them," reflected his belief in the importance of strategy and leadership in achieving military success.

Death

Suvorov died on May 18, 1800, at the age of 70, in the town of Saint Petersburg, Russia. His death marked the passing of one of Russia's greatest military leaders and a legendary figure in European military history. Suvorov was mourned by his soldiers, who regarded him as a father figure and a hero of the Russian nation.

In conclusion, Alexander Suvorov's legacy as one of Russia's greatest military commanders is a testament to his strategic brilliance, tactical innovation, and unwavering dedication to the art of war. His campaigns and victories on the battlefield earned him a reputation as one of the most successful and respected generals of his time, and his influence continues to be felt in military circles around the world. Suvorov's life and achievements serve as an inspiration to future generations of soldiers and leaders, reminding us of the timeless principles of courage, discipline, and determination that are essential for success in war and life.

50

Tamerlane (Timurid Empire)

Tamerlane, also known as Timur, was a formidable conqueror and founder of the Timurid Empire, which spanned much of Central Asia, Persia, and parts of the Middle East during the 14th and 15th centuries. Born into a noble Turkic-Mongol family in present-day Uzbekistan in 1336, Tamerlane rose from humble beginnings to become one of history's most ruthless and successful military leaders. His campaigns of conquest left a lasting impact on the regions he conquered, reshaping the geopolitical landscape of the time.

Birth

Tamerlane was born on April 9, 1336, in the city of Kesh (present-day Shahrisabz), located in the fertile valleys of modern-day Uzbekistan. His birth name was Timur, which means "iron" in the Turkic languages. He was born into the Barlas tribe, a Mongol clan that had settled in the region centuries earlier.

Early Life and Education

Little is known about Tamerlane's early life, but it is believed that he spent his youth herding sheep and cattle on the steppes of Central Asia. He received a rudimentary education in the arts of war and horsemanship, as well as in the customs and traditions of his Turkic-Mongol heritage.

Wars

Tamerlane's military career began in earnest in the early 1370s when he emerged as a powerful warlord in the wake of the collapse of the Mongol Empire. He quickly established himself as a formidable leader, uniting various Turkic and Mongol tribes under his banner and launching a series of campaigns to expand his territory.

One of Tamerlane's most famous campaigns was his invasion of Persia in 1381, where he defeated the Jalayirid Sultanate and established his dominance over much of the region. Over the next two decades, Tamerlane embarked on a series of conquests that would bring him into conflict with the rulers of neighboring empires, including the Golden Horde, the Ottoman Empire, and the Delhi Sultanate.

Overall Win and Lose

Tamerlane's military campaigns were marked by ruthless efficiency and brutal tactics, earning him a fearsome reputation as a conqueror. He was known for his strategic brilliance, tactical innovation, and ability to inspire loyalty and devotion among his troops. Despite facing formidable opponents and daunting logistical challenges, Tamerlane achieved remarkable success on the battlefield, expanding his empire to its greatest extent and establishing himself as one of the most powerful rulers of his time.

However, Tamerlane's conquests came at a great cost, destroying countless cities, the slaughter of millions of people, and the devastation entire regions. His campaigns were marked by unimaginable cruelty and brutality, earning him the epithet "Tamerlane the Great" among some, and "Tamerlane the Terrible" among others.

Interesting Facts and Figures

- Tamerlane was a master of psychological warfare, often employing terror and intimidation to subdue his enemies. He was known for his use of brutal tactics, such as building pyramids of severed heads and massacring entire populations, to instill fear and subjugate resistance.

- Despite his reputation as a ruthless conqueror, Tamerlane was also a patron of the arts and sciences, fostering a cultural renaissance in the cities of his empire. He established magnificent architectural monuments, commissioned lavish works of art, and promoted scholarship and learning among his subjects.
- Tamerlane's military campaigns were characterized by their speed, mobility, and flexibility. He relied heavily on cavalry units, particularly his elite corps of mounted archers known as the Timariots, to launch lightning-fast raids and surprise attacks against his enemies.

Death

Tamerlane died on February 18, 1405, in the city of Otrar, in present-day Kazakhstan, while on his way to launch yet another campaign of conquest. He was buried in a magnificent mausoleum in his capital city of Samarkand, which remains a symbol of his power and grandeur to this day.

In conclusion, Tamerlane's legacy as a conqueror and empire-builder is a complex and controversial one. While he is remembered as one of history's most successful military leaders, his conquests came at a great human cost and left a trail of destruction and suffering in their wake. Despite his ruthless methods and brutal tactics, Tamerlane's achievements in uniting and expanding the Timurid Empire cannot be denied, and his impact on the history of Central Asia and the Middle East is still felt to this day.

51

Tariq ibn Ziyad (Islamic Umayyad Caliphate)

Tariq ibn Ziyad, a celebrated military commander of the early Islamic era, played a pivotal role in the expansion of the Islamic Umayyad Caliphate into the Iberian Peninsula. His conquest of the region, known as the Umayyad conquest of Hispania, forever altered the course of history, leaving a lasting legacy that continues to influence the culture, language, and heritage of modern-day Spain and Portugal. Born in the Arabian Peninsula during the 7th century, Tariq's military exploits and strategic brilliance have earned him a revered place in Islamic history.

Birth

Tariq ibn Ziyad was born in 670 CE in the city of Taif, located in the western region of the Arabian Peninsula, which is now part of modern-day Saudi Arabia. Little is known about his early life or family background, but he likely grew up in a society deeply influenced by the teachings of Islam and the martial traditions of the Arab tribes.

Early Life and Education

As a young man, Tariq ibn Ziyad received a comprehensive education in the Quran, Islamic law, and the art of warfare. He honed his skills as a military leader and strategist through years of training and experience, rising through the ranks of the Arab armies during the early Islamic conquests.

Wars

Tariq ibn Ziyad's most famous military campaign was the conquest of the Iberian Peninsula, which began in 711 CE. At the time, the region was controlled by the Visigothic Kingdom, a Christian kingdom that had ruled over much of modern-day Spain and Portugal since the collapse of the Western Roman Empire.

Leading an army of Arab and Berber soldiers, Tariq crossed the Strait of Gibraltar in April 711 and landed on the Iberian Peninsula with a force of around 7,000 troops. His army faced stiff resistance from the Visigothic forces led by King Roderic, but Tariq's strategic brilliance and superior tactics enabled him to achieve a decisive victory at the Battle of Guadalete later that year.

Overall Win and Lose

Tariq ibn Ziyad's conquest of the Iberian Peninsula was a resounding success, laying the foundation for centuries of Islamic rule in the region. His victory at the Battle of Guadalete opened the door for further Arab-Berber incursions into Spain and Portugal, leading to the establishment of the Umayyad Emirate of Cordoba and the subsequent spread of Islam across the peninsula.

Despite his initial successes, Tariq's military career was not without its challenges. He faced opposition from rival factions within the Arab-Muslim world, as well as resistance from local populations in the territories he conquered. However, his strategic acumen, leadership skills, and unwavering determination enabled him to overcome these obstacles and secure his place in history as one of Islam's greatest military commanders.

Interesting Facts and Figures

- Tariq ibn Ziyad's conquest of the Iberian Peninsula is one of the most significant events in medieval history. It marked the beginning of centuries of Islamic rule in Spain and Portugal, during which the region became a center of Islamic culture, learning, and civilization.

- Tariq's name is forever linked with the Rock of Gibraltar, which he famously crossed with his army during the initial stages of the conquest. The name "Gibraltar" is derived from the Arabic phrase "Jabal Tariq," meaning "Tariq's Mountain."
- Tariq ibn Ziyad's conquest of Spain had far-reaching consequences for the region, including the spread of Islam, the introduction of Arabic language and culture, and the fusion of Arab, Berber, and European traditions.

Death

Tariq ibn Ziyad died in 720 CE, at the age of 50, in Damascus, the capital of the Umayyad Caliphate. Although his exact cause of death is unknown, his legacy as a military commander and conqueror continues to be remembered and celebrated by Muslims around the world.

In conclusion, Tariq ibn Ziyad's conquest of the Iberian Peninsula stands as one of the most significant events in Islamic history. His strategic brilliance, leadership skills, and unwavering determination enabled him to achieve a decisive victory that forever altered the course of history, leaving a lasting legacy that continues to influence the culture, language, and heritage of modern-day Spain and Portugal. Tariq's name remains synonymous with courage, determination, and the spirit of conquest, inspiring generations of Muslims to strive for greatness and achieve their goals.

52

Tecumseh (Shawnee)

Tecumseh, a legendary Shawnee leader, diplomat, and warrior, played a pivotal role in resisting the encroachment of European settlers and the expansion of the United States into Native American territories during the late 18th and early 19th centuries. Born into the Shawnee tribe in the Ohio Country in 1768, Tecumseh emerged as one of the most influential and charismatic Native American leaders of his time, advocating for unity among indigenous peoples and leading a coalition of tribes against American forces during the War of 1812.

Birth

Tecumseh was born in March 1768, in the Shawnee village of Pekowi, located in what is now present-day Ohio, United States. He was born into the Kispoko clan of the Shawnee tribe, which was one of the largest and most powerful Native American confederacies in the Ohio Valley region.

Early Life and Education

Little is known about Tecumseh's early life, but he likely received a traditional upbringing within the Shawnee community, learning the skills of hunting, fishing, and warfare from his elders. As a young man, Tecumseh distinguished himself as a skilled hunter and warrior, earning a reputation for his bravery, leadership, and tactical acumen.

Wars

Tecumseh's life was defined by his struggle to defend Native American lands and sovereignty against the encroachment of European settlers and the expansion of the United States. Throughout his career, Tecumseh led numerous military campaigns and diplomatic efforts to unite indigenous peoples and resist American expansionism.

One of Tecumseh's most notable achievements was the formation of a pan-Indian confederation known as the Tecumseh's Confederacy, which sought to unite Native American tribes in a common cause against American encroachment. Under Tecumseh's leadership, the confederation waged a series of battles against American forces, including the Battle of Tippecanoe in 1811, where Tecumseh's forces clashed with Indiana Territory Governor William Henry Harrison's army.

Overall Win and Lose

Tecumseh's efforts to unite Native American tribes against American expansion ultimately ended in defeat, as American forces, bolstered by superior numbers and resources, gradually pushed indigenous peoples further westward. Despite his tactical brilliance and charismatic leadership, Tecumseh was unable to overcome the overwhelming military power of the United States.

However, Tecumseh's legacy as a visionary leader and champion of indigenous rights continues to inspire Native American activists and leaders to this day. His efforts to unite Native American tribes in a common cause against American expansion laid the groundwork for future resistance movements and contributed to the ongoing struggle for indigenous sovereignty and self-determination.

Interesting Facts and Figures

- Tecumseh was known for his oratorical skills and ability to inspire his followers with his impassioned speeches. He traveled extensively throughout the Ohio Valley and the Great Lakes region, rallying support for his vision of a united Native American confederation.

- Tecumseh's name is often associated with the War of 1812, during which he allied himself with the British against the United States. He played a crucial role in several key battles of the war, including the capture of Detroit in 1812 and the Battle of the Thames in 1813.
- Tecumseh's death in the Battle of the Thames on October 5, 1813, marked the end of his efforts to resist American expansion and unite Native American tribes. His death was a significant blow to the indigenous peoples of North America, but his legacy as a fearless warrior and visionary leader lives on.

Death

Tecumseh was killed in the Battle of the Thames on October 5, 1813, near present-day Chatham-Kent, Ontario, Canada. His death dealt a severe blow to the Tecumseh Confederacy and the broader indigenous resistance movement, but his legacy as a courageous leader and advocate for indigenous rights endures to this day.

In conclusion, Tecumseh's life and legacy represent a powerful testament to the resilience, courage, and determination of Native American peoples in the face of overwhelming adversity. His efforts to unite indigenous tribes against American expansionism and defend their lands and sovereignty have left an indelible mark on the history of North America and continue to inspire generations of indigenous activists and leaders in their ongoing struggle for justice and equality.

53

Togo Heihachiro (Japan)

Togo Heihachiro, a towering figure in Japanese naval history, rose to prominence as one of the most skilled and respected admirals of his time. Born into a samurai family in 1848, Togo played a pivotal role in modernizing the Imperial Japanese Navy and securing Japan's status as a major maritime power. His decisive victory at the Battle of Tsushima during the Russo-Japanese War of 1904-1905 solidified his reputation as one of the greatest naval commanders in history.

Birth

Togo Heihachiro was born on January 27, 1848, in the Satsuma Domain, located in present-day Kagoshima Prefecture, Japan. He was born into a samurai family with a long tradition of military service, and from a young age, he displayed a keen interest in naval affairs and maritime strategy.

Early Life and Education

Togo received a traditional samurai education, which emphasized martial arts, military strategy, and the Confucian principles of loyalty, filial piety, and honor. He excelled in his studies and demonstrated a natural aptitude for naval warfare, which would shape his future career and accomplishments.

At the age of 14, Togo entered the Kagoshima Naval Training Center, where he received formal training in seamanship, navigation, and naval tactics. He quickly distinguished himself as a talented and ambitious young officer, earning the respect and admiration of his superiors and peers.

Wars

Togo Heihachiro's most famous military campaign was his leadership of the Imperial Japanese Navy during the Russo-Japanese War of 1904-1905. The conflict fought between the Empire of Japan and the Russian Empire, centered on rival territorial and strategic interests in East Asia, particularly in Korea and Manchuria.

One of the decisive moments of the war came in May 1905, when Togo led the Japanese fleet to a stunning victory over the Russian Baltic Fleet at the Battle of Tsushima. The battle, which took place in the waters between Korea and Japan, saw Togo employ innovative tactics and superior firepower to inflict a devastating defeat on the Russian navy.

Overall Win and Lose

Togo Heihachiro's victory at the Battle of Tsushima was a watershed moment in naval history and a decisive turning point in the Russo-Japanese War. His strategic brilliance, tactical ingenuity, and unwavering determination enabled him to overcome formidable odds and achieve a resounding victory that secured Japan's position as a major maritime power.

Despite his military successes, Togo faced significant challenges and setbacks throughout his career, including political rivalries within the Japanese government and criticism from foreign observers. However, his leadership, professionalism, and dedication to duty enabled him to overcome these obstacles and emerge as one of the most celebrated figures in Japanese history.

Interesting Facts and Figures

- Togo Heihachiro was known for his strict discipline and attention to detail, which he instilled in his officers and crews through rigorous training and drills. His emphasis on professionalism and preparedness contributed to the Imperial Japanese Navy's reputation as one of the most formidable naval forces of its time.

- Togo's victory at the Battle of Tsushima solidified his reputation as one of the greatest naval commanders in history and earned him the admiration of his peers and adversaries alike. He became a national hero in Japan and was celebrated as the "Nelson of the East" for his naval prowess and leadership.
- Togo Heihachiro's legacy continues to be honored in Japan today, with numerous monuments, memorials, and museums dedicated to his memory. His contributions to the modernization and expansion of the Imperial Japanese Navy have had a lasting impact on Japan's maritime strategy and defense posture.

Death

Togo Heihachiro died on May 30, 1934, at the age of 86, in Tokyo, Japan. His death marked the passing of one of Japan's greatest naval heroes and a legendary figure in the annals of maritime history. He was posthumously honored with numerous awards and accolades, including the Order of the Chrysanthemum, Japan's highest honor.

In conclusion, Togo Heihachiro's life and career exemplify the virtues of leadership, courage, and dedication to duty. His decisive victory at the Battle of Tsushima propelled Japan onto the world stage as a major naval power and secured his place in history as one of the greatest admirals of all time. Togo's legacy continues to inspire generations of naval officers and maritime leaders, serving as a testament to the enduring impact of his achievements on Japan and the world.

54

Toussaint Louverture (Haiti)

Toussaint Louverture, born François-Dominique Toussaint, is a towering figure in the history of Haiti and the fight against slavery. Born into slavery, Toussaint rose to become a revolutionary leader and the principal architect of Haiti's independence from French colonial rule. His leadership, strategic genius and unwavering commitment to freedom inspired a nation and left an indelible mark on the struggle for human rights and equality worldwide.

Birth

Toussaint Louverture was born into slavery on May 20, 1743, on the Breda plantation in Saint-Domingue, a French colony on the island of Hispaniola, which is now modern-day Haiti. His exact parentage and early life are uncertain, but he is believed to have been the son of enslaved Africans who had been brought to the colony to work on the sugar plantations.

Early Life and Education

Despite being born into slavery, Toussaint was fortunate to receive some education during his youth. He learned to read and write, acquiring knowledge of French and gaining familiarity with the principles of Enlightenment philosophy. His intelligence and aptitude for learning set him apart from many of his enslaved peers and would later play a crucial role in his leadership.

As a young man, Toussaint worked as a coachman and steward on the plantation, where he gained valuable experience and honed his skills as a leader and organizer. He also developed a deep-seated resentment of the institution of slavery and a burning desire for freedom and justice.

Wars

Toussaint Louverture's rise to prominence came during the Haitian Revolution, a tumultuous period of upheaval and resistance against French colonial rule in Saint-Domingue. Inspired by the ideals of the French Revolution and fueled by a desire for liberty and equality, Toussaint emerged as a charismatic and visionary leader of the enslaved population.

His military career began in 1791, when a slave revolt erupted in Saint-Domingue, leading to a protracted and bloody conflict between the enslaved Africans and the French colonial authorities. Toussaint quickly distinguished himself as a skilled tactician and strategist, leading guerrilla warfare campaigns against the French and their allies.

One of Toussaint's most significant military achievements was his alliance with the Spanish, British, and American forces against the French during the Haitian Revolution. His diplomatic skill and military prowess enabled him to outmaneuver his adversaries and secure significant territorial gains for the revolutionary cause.

Overall Win and Lose

Toussaint Louverture's leadership and military genius played a decisive role in the success of the Haitian Revolution, culminating in the establishment of Haiti as the first independent black republic in the Western Hemisphere in 1804. His victory over the forces of slavery and colonial oppression inspired enslaved peoples around the world and dealt a significant blow to the institution of slavery.

However, Toussaint's vision of a free and independent Haiti was short-lived, as internal divisions and external pressures led to political instability and conflict within the new nation. In 1802, Toussaint was betrayed by the French and captured by their forces. He was subsequently deported to France, where he died in captivity in 1803, leaving behind a legacy of courage, resilience, and defiance.

Interesting Facts and Figures

- Toussaint Louverture was known for his exceptional leadership qualities, including his ability to inspire loyalty and devotion among his followers. He was revered as a father figure and a symbol of hope and freedom for the enslaved population of Haiti.
- Toussaint's military campaigns were marked by their strategic brilliance and tactical innovation. He employed guerrilla warfare tactics, scorched-earth policies, and psychological warfare techniques to undermine the strength and morale of his enemies.
- Toussaint was also a skilled administrator and statesman, overseeing the development of Haiti's economy, infrastructure, and institutions during his tenure as governor-general. He implemented agricultural reforms, built roads and bridges, and established schools and hospitals for the benefit of all Haitians.

Death

Toussaint Louverture died in captivity on April 7, 1803, at Fort-de-Joux, a mountain fortress in the French Alps. His death was a tragic end to a remarkable life, but his legacy as a freedom fighter and champion of human rights lives on in the hearts and minds of people everywhere.

In conclusion, Toussaint Louverture's life and legacy represent a triumph of the human spirit over oppression and injustice. His leadership and courage inspired a nation to rise against tyranny and oppression, leading to the establishment of Haiti as the first independent black republic in the Western Hemisphere. Toussaint's legacy continues to inspire generations of freedom fighters and social justice activists around the world, serving as a reminder of the enduring power of hope, resilience, and the quest for freedom.

55

William the Conqueror (Normandy/England)

William the Conqueror, also known as William I, was a medieval ruler who left an indelible mark on the history of England and Europe. Born in Normandy in 1028, he ascended to the throne of England in 1066 after his victory at the Battle of Hastings, marking the beginning of Norman rule in England. William's reign was characterized by significant political, social, and cultural changes, including the introduction of feudalism and the compilation of the Domesday Book. His legacy as a conqueror and statesman continues to shape the course of English history to this day.

Birth

William was born in Falaise, Normandy, in 1028, the illegitimate son of Robert I, Duke of Normandy, and his mistress, Herleva. Despite his illegitimate birth, William was recognized as Robert's heir and was groomed for leadership from a young age. He received a thorough education in military strategy, governance, and diplomacy, preparing him for the challenges of ruling a medieval kingdom.

Early Life and Education

William's childhood was marked by political instability and dynastic struggles within the Duchy of Normandy. Following his father's death in 1035, William faced numerous challenges to his claim to the ducal throne, including rebellion from powerful Norman barons and external threats from neighboring rivals.

Despite these challenges, William proved himself to be a capable and determined leader, demonstrating his military prowess in battles against rebellious vassals and rival claimants to the ducal throne. By the time he reached adulthood, William had firmly established himself as the undisputed ruler of Normandy, consolidating his power through a combination of diplomacy, military force, and strategic alliances.

Wars

William's most famous military campaign was his invasion of England in 1066, which culminated in his decisive victory at the Battle of Hastings. The invasion was prompted by William's claim to the English throne, which he based on his purported designation as heir by his distant cousin, King Edward the Confessor of England.

Upon Edward's death in January 1066, the English throne was claimed by Harold Godwinson, the powerful Earl of Wessex, who was crowned King Harold II shortly thereafter. William disputed Harold's claim, asserting his right to the throne as Edward's designated successor.

The stage was set for a confrontation between the two claimants, and in September 1066, William assembled a formidable army of Norman knights, mercenaries, and infantry and set sail for England. On October 14, 1066, the two armies met at the Battle of Hastings, where William's forces emerged victorious after a day of intense fighting. The battle proved to be a turning point in English history, marking the beginning of Norman rule in England and the end of Anglo-Saxon dominance.

Overall Win and Lose

William's conquest of England was a resounding success, establishing him as the first Norman king of England and laying the foundation for the Norman Conquest, which transformed the political, social, and cultural landscape of England. His victory at Hastings secured his hold on the English throne and paved the way for the consolidation of Norman power throughout the realm.

However, William's reign was not without its challenges and setbacks. He faced numerous rebellions and uprisings from disgruntled Anglo-Saxon nobles and native English populations who resented Norman rule. Despite these challenges, William proved to be a shrewd and ruthless ruler, employing a combination of military force, political intrigue, and administrative reforms to maintain control over his new kingdom.

Interesting Facts and Figures

- One of the most enduring legacies of William's reign is the compilation of the Domesday Book, a comprehensive survey of landholdings and property ownership in England. Completed in 1086, the Domesday Book provided invaluable information about the wealth and resources of the kingdom and helped William administer his realm more effectively.
- William's conquest of England had far-reaching consequences for English society and culture. The Norman Conquest introduced a new ruling elite of Norman nobles and knights, who brought with them their language, customs, and traditions. The fusion of Norman and Anglo-Saxon influences laid the groundwork for the development of the English language and identity.
- William's reign also saw the construction of numerous castles, fortifications, and religious buildings throughout England, including the Tower of London, which served as a symbol of Norman power and authority. These structures played a crucial role in consolidating Norman's control over the kingdom and maintaining order in the face of resistance and rebellion.

Death

William the Conqueror died on September 9, 1087, at the age of 59, at the Priory of Saint Gervase near Rouen, Normandy. His death marked the end of an era and the beginning of a new chapter in English history. He was succeeded by his son William Rufus as King of England, who continued his father's policies of centralization and consolidation of royal power.

In conclusion, William the Conqueror's reign was a pivotal period in English history, marking the transition from Anglo-Saxon to Norman rule and laying the foundation for the development of the English nation-state. His conquest of England and establishment of Norman rule had profound and lasting consequences for English society, culture, and governance, shaping the course of English history for centuries to come.